BUSINESS EMERGENCY CONTACTS

BUSINESS INFORMATION

BUSINESS NAME	
FACILITY NAME	
ADDRESS	
FACILITY PHONE 1	
FACILITY PHONE 2	

EMERGENCY NUMBERS

FIRE DEPT	
POLICE DEPT	
AMBULANCE SVC	
HOSPITAL	
POISON CONTROL	
ALARM COMPANY	

UTILITY COMPANIES

NATURAL GAS	
ELECTRICITY	
WATER SVC	

INSURANCE COMPANY

COMPANY NAME	
CLAIMS HOTLINE	
POLICY NUMBER	

UPDATE INFORMATION

UPDATED BY	
DATE OF UPDATE	

FACILITY MANAGERS

NAME	PRIMARY CONTACT #	ALTERNATE #

EMPLOYEES

NAME	PRIMARY CONTACT #	ALTERNATE #

2021

JANUARY
SUN	MON	TUE	WED	THU	FRI	SAT
					1	2
3	4	5	6	7	8	9
10	11	12	13	14	15	16
17	18	19	20	21	22	23
24	25	26	27	28	29	30
31						

FEBRUARY
SUN	MON	TUE	WED	THU	FRI	SAT
	1	2	3	4	5	6
7	8	9	10	11	12	13
14	15	16	17	18	19	20
21	22	23	24	25	26	27
28						

MARCH
SUN	MON	TUE	WED	THU	FRI	SAT
	1	2	3	4	5	6
7	8	9	10	11	12	13
14	15	16	17	18	19	20
21	22	23	24	25	26	27
28	29	30	31			

APRIL
SUN	MON	TUE	WED	THU	FRI	SAT
				1	2	3
4	5	6	7	8	9	10
11	12	13	14	15	16	17
18	19	20	21	22	23	24
25	26	27	28	29	30	

MAY
SUN	MON	TUE	WED	THU	FRI	SAT
						1
2	3	4	5	6	7	8
9	10	11	12	13	14	15
16	17	18	19	20	21	22
23	24	25	26	27	28	29
30	31					

JUNE
SUN	MON	TUE	WED	THU	FRI	SAT
		1	2	3	4	5
6	7	8	9	10	11	12
13	14	15	16	17	18	19
20	21	22	23	24	25	26
27	28	29	30			

JULY
SUN	MON	TUE	WED	THU	FRI	SAT
				1	2	3
4	5	6	7	8	9	10
11	12	13	14	15	16	17
18	19	20	21	22	23	24
25	26	27	28	29	30	31

AUGUST
SUN	MON	TUE	WED	THU	FRI	SAT
1	2	3	4	5	6	7
8	9	10	11	12	13	14
15	16	17	18	19	20	21
22	23	24	25	26	27	28
29	30	31				

SEPTEMBER
SUN	MON	TUE	WED	THU	FRI	SAT
			1	2	3	4
5	6	7	8	9	10	11
12	13	14	15	16	17	18
19	20	21	22	23	24	25
26	27	28	29	30		

OCTOBER
SUN	MON	TUE	WED	THU	FRI	SAT
					1	2
3	4	5	6	7	8	9
10	11	12	13	14	15	16
17	18	19	20	21	22	23
24	25	26	27	28	29	30
31						

NOVEMBER
SUN	MON	TUE	WED	THU	FRI	SAT
	1	2	3	4	5	6
7	8	9	10	11	12	13
14	15	16	17	18	19	20
21	22	23	24	25	26	27
28	29	30				

DECEMBER
SUN	MON	TUE	WED	THU	FRI	SAT
			1	2	3	4
5	6	7	8	9	10	11
12	13	14	15	16	17	18
19	20	21	22	23	24	25
26	27	28	29	30	31	

2022

JANUARY
SUN	MON	TUE	WED	THU	FRI	SAT
						1
2	3	4	5	6	7	8
9	10	11	12	13	14	15
16	17	18	19	20	21	22
23	24	25	26	27	28	29
30	31					

FEBRUARY
SUN	MON	TUE	WED	THU	FRI	SAT
		1	2	3	4	5
6	7	8	9	10	11	12
13	14	15	16	17	18	19
20	21	22	23	24	25	26
27	28					

MARCH
SUN	MON	TUE	WED	THU	FRI	SAT
		1	2	3	4	5
6	7	8	9	10	11	12
13	14	15	16	17	18	19
20	21	22	23	24	25	26
27	28	29	30	31		

APRIL
SUN	MON	TUE	WED	THU	FRI	SAT
					1	2
3	4	5	6	7	8	9
10	11	12	13	14	15	16
17	18	19	20	21	22	23
24	25	26	27	28	29	30

MAY
SUN	MON	TUE	WED	THU	FRI	SAT
1	2	3	4	5	6	7
8	9	10	11	12	13	14
15	16	17	18	19	20	21
22	23	24	25	26	27	28
29	30	31				

JUNE
SUN	MON	TUE	WED	THU	FRI	SAT
			1	2	3	4
5	6	7	8	9	10	11
12	13	14	15	16	17	18
19	20	21	22	23	24	25
26	27	28	29	30		

JULY
SUN	MON	TUE	WED	THU	FRI	SAT
					1	2
3	4	5	6	7	8	9
10	11	12	13	14	15	16
17	18	19	20	21	22	23
24	25	26	27	28	29	30
31						

AUGUST
SUN	MON	TUE	WED	THU	FRI	SAT
	1	2	3	4	5	6
7	8	9	10	11	12	13
14	15	16	17	18	19	20
21	22	23	24	25	26	27
28	29	30	31			

SEPTEMBER
SUN	MON	TUE	WED	THU	FRI	SAT
				1	2	3
4	5	6	7	8	9	10
11	12	13	14	15	16	17
18	19	20	21	22	23	24
25	26	27	28	29	30	

OCTOBER
SUN	MON	TUE	WED	THU	FRI	SAT
						1
2	3	4	5	6	7	8
9	10	11	12	13	14	15
16	17	18	19	20	21	22
23	24	25	26	27	28	29
30						

NOVEMBER
SUN	MON	TUE	WED	THU	FRI	SAT
		1	2	3	4	5
6	7	8	9	10	11	12
13	14	15	16	17	18	19
20	21	22	23	24	25	26
27	28	29	30			

DECEMBER
SUN	MON	TUE	WED	THU	FRI	SAT
				1	2	3
4	5	6	7	8	9	10
11	12	13	14	15	16	17
18	19	20	21	22	23	24
25	26	27	28	29	30	

HIVE INSPECTION SHEET

Apiary Location: _____
Hive ID: _____
Date and Time of Inspection: __ / __ / __   __ : __

INSPECTION DETAILS

Pollen Gathering: ____   Nectar Flow: ____   Weather: _____

Purpose for Inspection

DEVELOPMENT TIMES FOR HONEY BEE

Development (days)	Queen	Worker	Drones
Egg hatches after	3	3	3
Cells Capped after	8	8	10
Adults emerge after	16	21	24

HIVE STATUS

Queen Seen: ____   Marked: ____   Eggs: ____

Queen Cells with Egg, Larva or Pupa	Removed Queen Cells	* Queen Cells Remaining
Emergency	Spotty Drone Brood	* Frames with Brood
Swarm	Worker Brood in All Stages	* Frames of Honey/Nectar
Supersedure	Compact Brood Pattern	* Frames of Pollen
* Frames bees occupy in brood chamber	* Frames of Foundation	* Frames Open Comb
	* Supers in place	* Supers added

HEALTH

Signs of Disease: ____   Good Temper: ____
Small Hive Beetle Damage: ____
Nosema Streaking: ____
Signs of Varroa Mite Infestation: ____

Feeding and/or Medication:

ACTIONS TAKEN AND NOTES

COLONY CONDITION

Weak: ____   Marginal: ____   Strong: ____

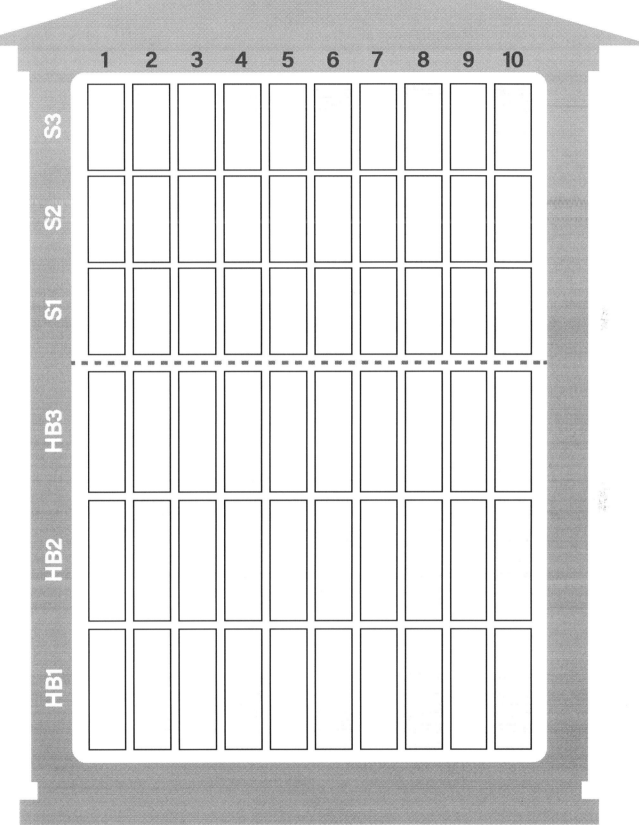

Indicate areas occupied by bees, honey, nectar and pollen. Show the location of vital Queen Cells

HIVE INSPECTION SHEET

Apiary Location: _____
Date and Time of Inspection: ___/___/___ ___:___
Hive ID: _____

INSPECTION DETAILS

Pollen Gathering: ___ **Nectar Flow:** ___ **Weather:** ___

Purpose for Inspection

DEVELOPMENT TIMES FOR HONEY BEE

Development (days)	Queen	Worker	Drones
Egg hatches after	3	3	3
Cells Capped after	8	8	10
Adults emerge after	16	21	24

HIVE STATUS

Queen Seen ___ Marked ___ Eggs ___

Queen Cells with Egg, Larva or Pupa	Removed Queen Cells	* Queen Cells Remaining
Emergency	Spotty Drone Brood	* Frames with Brood
Swarm	Worker Brood in All Stages	* Frames of Honey/Nectar
Supersedure	Compact Brood Pattern	* Frames of Pollen
* Frames bees occupy in brood chamber	* Frames of Foundation	* Frames Open Comb
	* Supers in place	* Supers added

HEALTH

Signs of Disease ___ Good Temper ___
Small Hive Beetle Damage ___
Nosema Streaking ___
Signs of Varroa Mite Infestation ___

Feeding and/or Medication

ACTIONS TAKEN AND NOTES

COLONY CONDITION

Weak ___ Marginal ___ Strong ___

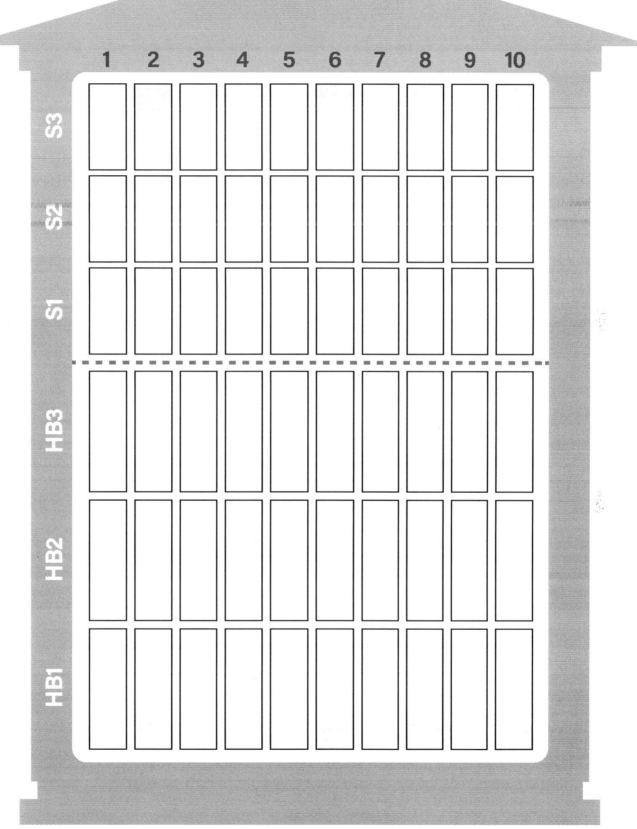

Indicate areas occupied by bees, honey, nectar and pollen. Show the location of vital Queen Cells

HIVE INSPECTION SHEET

Apiary Location	
Date and Time of Inspection	/ / :

Hive ID

INSPECTION DETAILS

Pollen Gathering		Nectar Flow		Weather	

Purpose for Inspection

DEVELOPMENT TIMES FOR HONEY BEE

Development (days)	Queen	Worker	Drones
Egg hatches after	3	3	3
Cells Capped after	8	8	10
Adults emerge after	16	21	24

HIVE STATUS

Queen Seen		Marked		Eggs	

Queen Cells with Egg, Larva or Pupa	Removed Queen Cells	* Queen Cells Remaining
	Spotty Drone Brood	* Frames with Brood
Emergency	Worker Brood in All Stages	* Frames of Honey/Nectar
Swarm	Compact Brood Pattern	* Frames of Pollen
Supersedure	* Frames of Foundation	* Frames Open Comb
* Frames bees occupy in brood chamber	* Supers in place	* Supers added

HEALTH

Signs of Disease		Good Temper	

Small Hive Beetle Damage

Nosema Streaking

Signs of Varroa Mite Infestation

Feeding and/or Medication

ACTIONS TAKEN AND NOTES

COLONY CONDITION

Weak		Marginal		Strong	

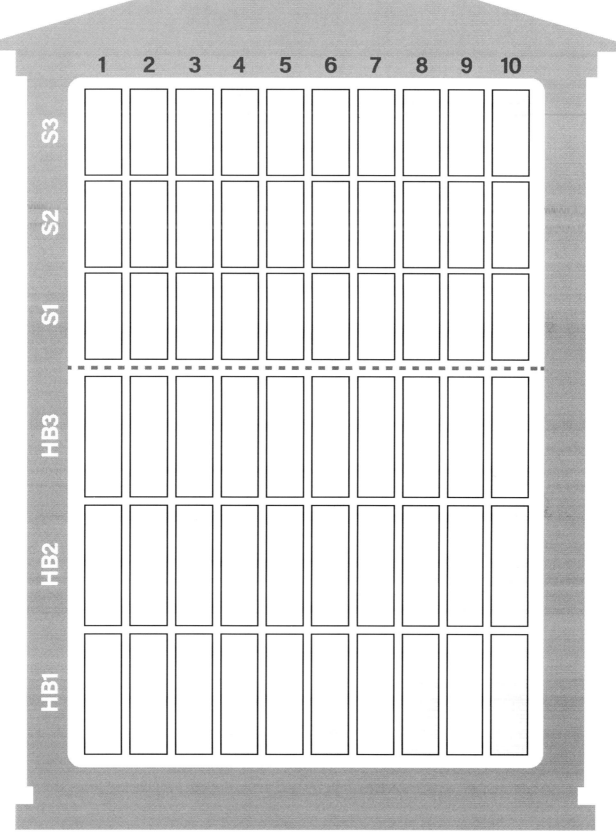

Indicate areas occupied by bees, honey, nectar and pollen. Show the location of vital Queen Cells

HIVE INSPECTION SHEET

Apiary Location:
Hive ID:
Date and Time of Inspection: /   /   :

INSPECTION DETAILS

Pollen Gathering: Nectar Flow: Weather:

Purpose for Inspection

DEVELOPMENT TIMES FOR HONEY BEE

Development (days)	Queen	Worker	Drones
Egg hatches after	3	3	3
Cells Capped after	8	8	10
Adults emerge after	16	21	24

HIVE STATUS

Queen Seen: Marked: Eggs:

Queen Cells with Egg, Larva or Pupa	Removed Queen Cells	* Queen Cells Remaining
Emergency	Spotty Drone Brood	* Frames with Brood
Swarm	Worker Brood in All Stages	* Frames of Honey/Nectar
Supersedure	Compact Brood Pattern	* Frames of Pollen
* Frames bees occupy in brood chamber	* Frames of Foundation	* Frames Open Comb
	* Supers in place	* Supers added

HEALTH

Signs of Disease: Good Temper:
Small Hive Beetle Damage:
Nosema Streaking:
Signs of Varroa Mite Infestation:

Feeding and/or Medication:

ACTIONS TAKEN AND NOTES

COLONY CONDITION

Weak: Marginal: Strong:

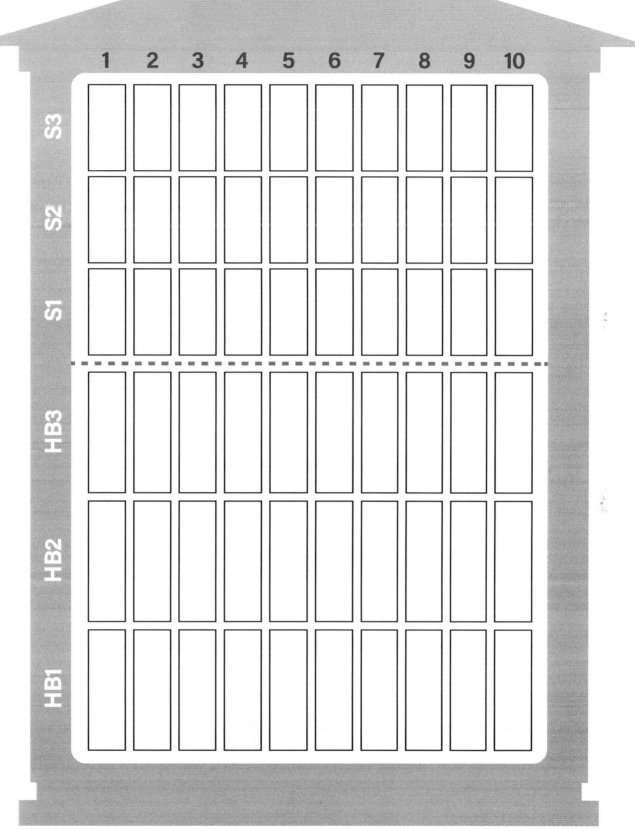

Indicate areas occupied by bees, honey, nectar and pollen. Show the location of vital Queen Cells

HIVE INSPECTION SHEET

Apiary Location: _____   Hive ID: _____

Date and Time of Inspection: __ / __ / __   __ : __

INSPECTION DETAILS

Pollen Gathering: ____   Nectar Flow: ____   Weather: _____

Purpose for Inspection

DEVELOPMENT TIMES FOR HONEY BEE

Development (days)	Queen	Worker	Drones
Egg hatches after	3	3	3
Cells Capped after	8	8	10
Adults emerge after	16	21	24

HIVE STATUS

Queen Seen: ____   Marked: ____   Eggs: ____

- Queen Cells with Egg, Larva or Pupa: ____
- Removed Queen Cells: ____
- * Queen Cells Remaining: ____
- Emergency: ____
- Spotty Drone Brood: ____
- * Frames with Brood: ____
- Swarm: ____
- Worker Brood in All Stages: ____
- * Frames of Honey/Nectar: ____
- Supersedure: ____
- Compact Brood Pattern: ____
- * Frames of Pollen: ____
- * Frames bees occupy in brood chamber: ____
- * Frames of Foundation: ____
- * Frames Open Comb: ____
- * Supers in place: ____
- * Supers added: ____

HEALTH

- Signs of Disease: ____   Good Temper: ____
- Small Hive Beetle Damage: ____
- Nosema Streaking: ____
- Signs of Varroa Mite Infestation: ____
- Feeding and/or Medication: _____

ACTIONS TAKEN AND NOTES

COLONY CONDITION

Weak: ____   Marginal: ____   Strong: ____

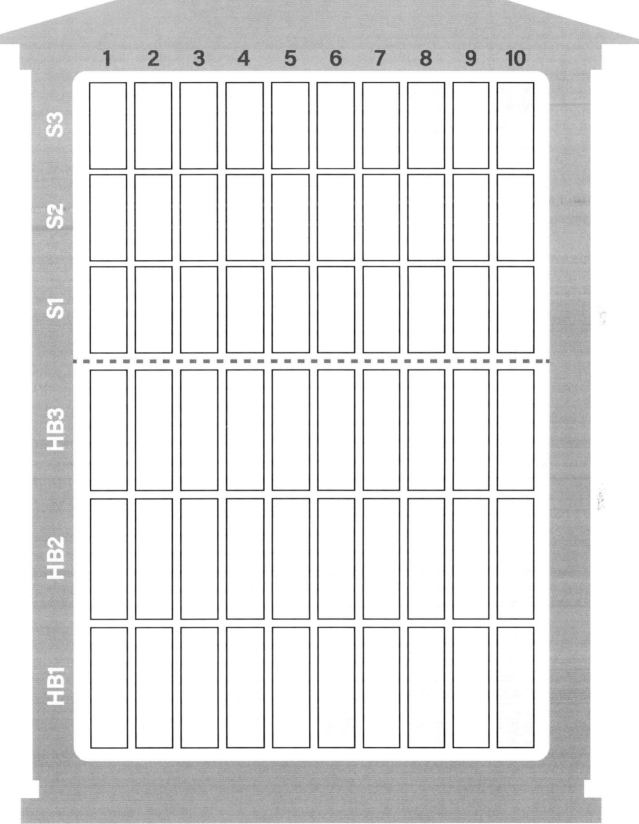

Indicate areas occupied by bees, honey, nectar and pollen. Show the location of vital Queen Cells

HIVE INSPECTION SHEET

Apiary Location		Hive ID	
Date and Time of Inspection	/ / :		

INSPECTION DETAILS

Pollen Gathering		Nectar Flow		Weather	

Purpose for Inspection

DEVELOPMENT TIMES FOR HONEY BEE

Development (days)	Queen	Worker	Drones
Egg hatches after	3	3	3
Cells Capped after	8	8	10
Adults emerge after	16	21	24

HIVE STATUS

Queen Seen		Marked		Eggs	

Queen Cells with Egg, Larva or Pupa		Removed Queen Cells		* Queen Cells Remaining	
		Spotty Drone Brood		* Frames with Brood	
Emergency		Worker Brood in All Stages		* Frames of Honey/Nectar	
Swarm		Compact Brood Pattern		* Frames of Pollen	
Supersedure		* Frames of Foundation		* Frames Open Comb	
* Frames bees occupy in brood chamber		* Supers in place		* Supers added	

HEALTH

Signs of Disease		Good Temper	
Small Hive Beetle Damage			
Nosema Streaking			
Signs of Varroa Mite Infestation			

Feeding and/or Medication

ACTIONS TAKEN AND NOTES

COLONY CONDITION

Weak		Marginal		Strong	

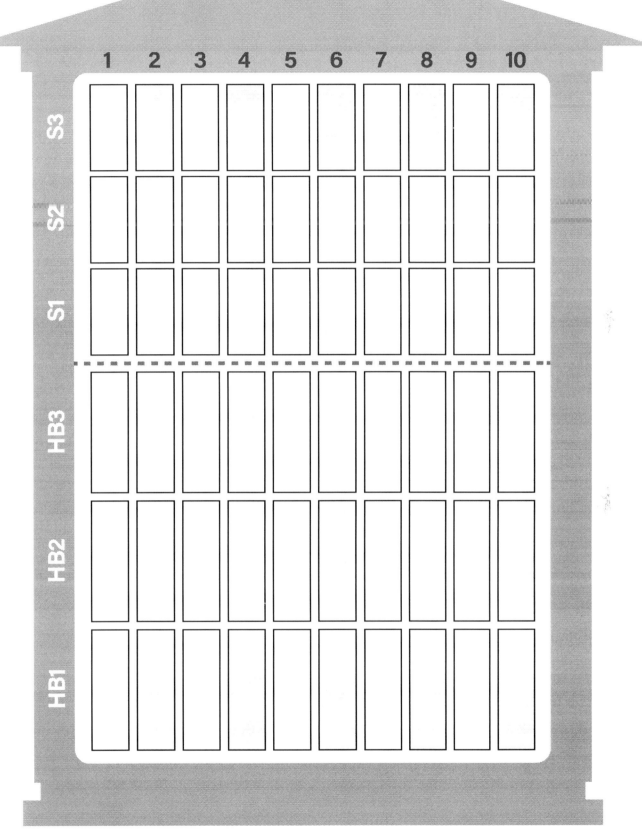

Indicate areas occupied by bees, honey, nectar and pollen. Show the location of vital Queen Cells

HIVE INSPECTION SHEET

Apiary Location:
Hive ID:
Date and Time of Inspection: / /   :

INSPECTION DETAILS

Pollen Gathering:
Nectar Flow:
Weather:

Purpose for Inspection

DEVELOPMENT TIMES FOR HONEY BEE

Development (days)	Queen	Worker	Drones
Egg hatches after	3	3	3
Cells Capped after	8	8	10
Adults emerge after	16	21	24

HIVE STATUS

Queen Seen: Marked: Eggs:

- Queen Cells with Egg, Larva or Pupa
- Removed Queen Cells
- * Queen Cells Remaining
- Emergency
- Spotty Drone Brood
- * Frames with Brood
- Swarm
- Worker Brood in All Stages
- * Frames of Honey/Nectar
- Supersedure
- Compact Brood Pattern
- * Frames of Pollen
- * Frames bees occupy in brood chamber
- * Frames of Foundation
- * Frames Open Comb
- * Supers in place
- * Supers added

HEALTH

- Signs of Disease
- Good Temper
- Small Hive Beetle Damage
- Nosema Streaking
- Signs of Varroa Mite Infestation
- Feeding and/or Medication

ACTIONS TAKEN AND NOTES

COLONY CONDITION

Weak   Marginal   Strong

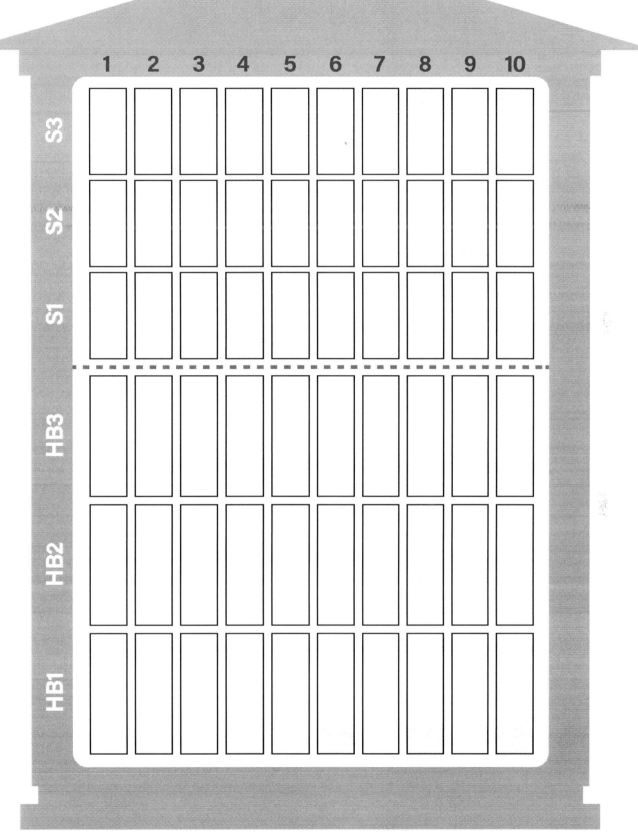

Indicate areas occupied by bees, honey, nectar and pollen. Show the location of vital Queen Cells

HIVE INSPECTION SHEET

Apiary Location: _____
Hive ID: _____
Date and Time of Inspection: __/__/__ __:__

INSPECTION DETAILS

Pollen Gathering: ____ Nectar Flow: ____ Weather: _____

Purpose for Inspection

DEVELOPMENT TIMES FOR HONEY BEE

Development (days)	Queen	Worker	Drones
Egg hatches after	3	3	3
Cells Capped after	8	8	10
Adults emerge after	16	21	24

HIVE STATUS

Queen Seen: ____ Marked: ____ Eggs: ____

Queen Cells with Egg, Larva or Pupa	Removed Queen Cells	* Queen Cells Remaining
Emergency	Spotty Drone Brood	* Frames with Brood
Swarm	Worker Brood in All Stages	* Frames of Honey/Nectar
Supersedure	Compact Brood Pattern	* Frames of Pollen
* Frames bees occupy in brood chamber	* Frames of Foundation	* Frames Open Comb
	* Supers in place	* Supers added

HEALTH

Signs of Disease: ____ Good Temper: ____
Small Hive Beetle Damage: ____
Nosema Streaking: ____
Signs of Varroa Mite Infestation: ____

Feeding and/or Medication:

ACTIONS TAKEN AND NOTES

COLONY CONDITION

Weak: ____ Marginal: ____ Strong: ____

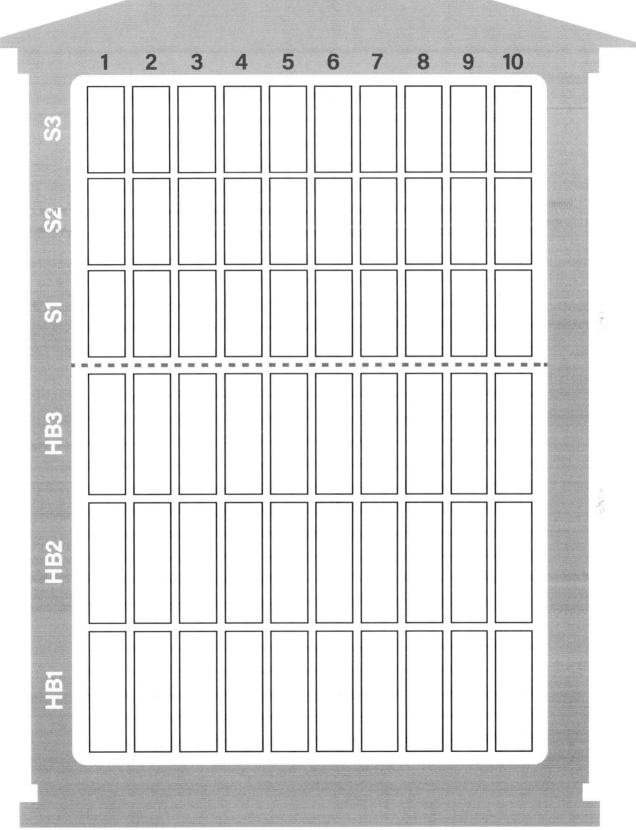

Indicate areas occupied by bees, honey, nectar and pollen. Show the location of vital Queen Cells

HIVE INSPECTION SHEET

Apiary Location: _____ Hive ID: _____
Date and Time of Inspection: __/__/__ : __

INSPECTION DETAILS

Pollen Gathering: ____ Nectar Flow: ____ Weather: _____

Purpose for Inspection

DEVELOPMENT TIMES FOR HONEY BEE

Development (days)	Queen	Worker	Drones
Egg hatches after	3	3	3
Cells Capped after	8	8	10
Adults emerge after	16	21	24

HIVE STATUS

Queen Seen: ____ Marked: ____ Eggs: ____

Queen Cells with Egg, Larva or Pupa	Removed Queen Cells	* Queen Cells Remaining
	Spotty Drone Brood	* Frames with Brood
Emergency	Worker Brood in All Stages	* Frames of Honey/Nectar
Swarm	Compact Brood Pattern	* Frames of Pollen
Supersedure	* Frames of Foundation	* Frames Open Comb
* Frames bees occupy in brood chamber	* Supers in place	* Supers added

HEALTH

Signs of Disease: ____ Good Temper: ____
Small Hive Beetle Damage: ____
Nosema Streaking: ____
Signs of Varroa Mite Infestation: ____

Feeding and/or Medication: _____

ACTIONS TAKEN AND NOTES

COLONY CONDITION

Weak: ____ Marginal: ____ Strong: ____

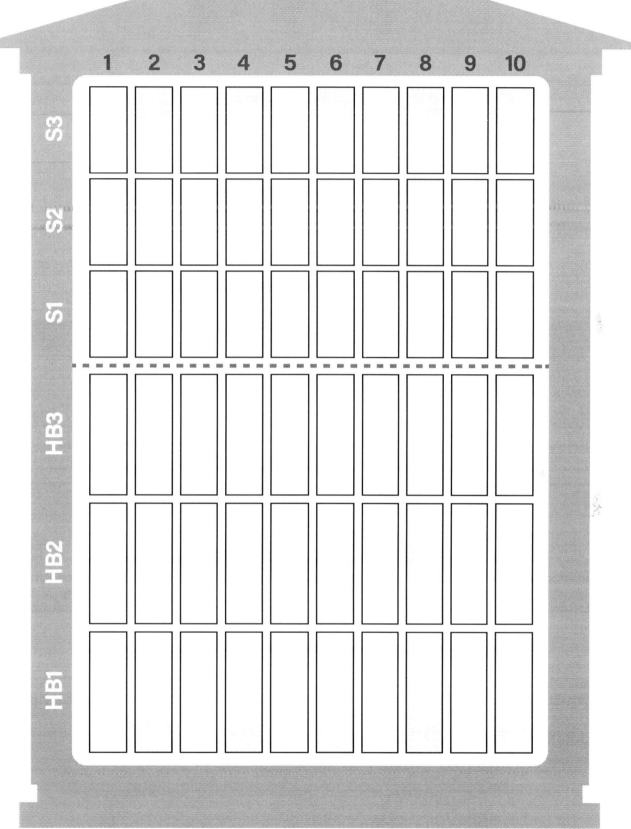

Indicate areas occupied by bees, honey, nectar and pollen. Show the location of vital Queen Cells

HIVE INSPECTION SHEET

Apiary Location: _____
Hive ID: _____
Date and Time of Inspection: ___/___/___   ___:___

INSPECTION DETAILS

Pollen Gathering: ___   **Nectar Flow:** ___   **Weather:** _____

Purpose for Inspection

_____

DEVELOPMENT TIMES FOR HONEY BEE

Development (days)	Queen	Worker	Drones
Egg hatches after	3	3	3
Cells Capped after	8	8	10
Adults emerge after	16	21	24

HIVE STATUS

Queen Seen: ___   **Marked:** ___   **Eggs:** ___

Queen Cells with Egg, Larva or Pupa	Removed Queen Cells	* Queen Cells Remaining
Emergency	Spotty Drone Brood	* Frames with Brood
Swarm	Worker Brood in All Stages	* Frames of Honey/Nectar
Supersedure	Compact Brood Pattern	* Frames of Pollen
* Frames bees occupy in brood chamber	* Frames of Foundation	* Frames Open Comb
	* Supers in place	* Supers added

HEALTH

Signs of Disease: ___   **Good Temper:** ___
Small Hive Beetle Damage: ___
Nosema Streaking: ___
Signs of Varroa Mite Infestation: ___

Feeding and/or Medication

_____

ACTIONS TAKEN AND NOTES

_____

COLONY CONDITION

Weak: ___   **Marginal:** ___   **Strong:** ___

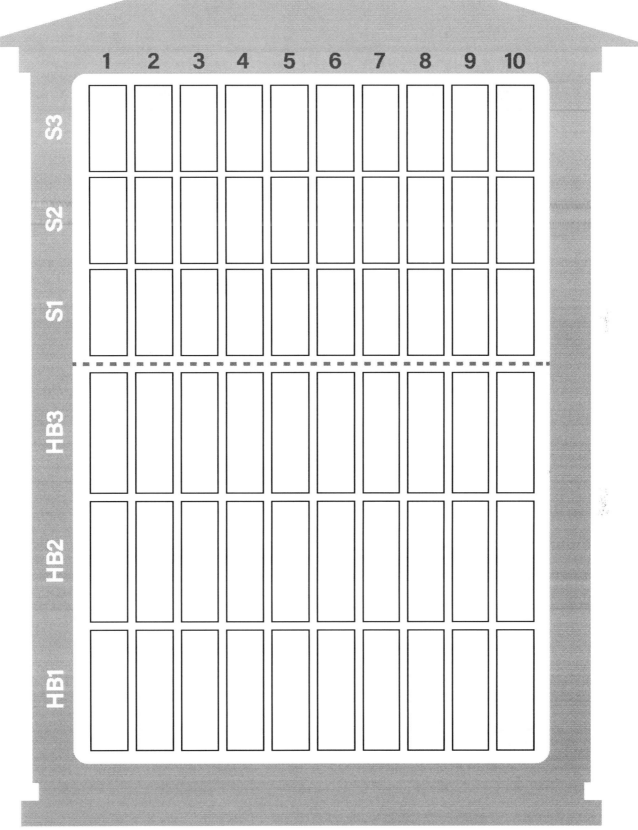

Indicate areas occupied by bees, honey, nectar and pollen. Show the location of vital Queen Cells

HIVE INSPECTION SHEET

Apiary Location: _____

Hive ID: _____

Date and Time of Inspection: __/__/__ __:__

INSPECTION DETAILS

Pollen Gathering: ___ Nectar Flow: ___ Weather: _____

Purpose for Inspection

DEVELOPMENT TIMES FOR HONEY BEE

Development (days)	Queen	Worker	Drones
Egg hatches after	3	3	3
Cells Capped after	8	8	10
Adults emerge after	16	21	24

HIVE STATUS

Queen Seen: ___ Marked: ___ Eggs: ___

Queen Cells with Egg, Larva or Pupa	Removed Queen Cells	* Queen Cells Remaining
Emergency	Spotty Drone Brood	* Frames with Brood
Swarm	Worker Brood in All Stages	* Frames of Honey/Nectar
Supersedure	Compact Brood Pattern	* Frames of Pollen
* Frames bees occupy in brood chamber	* Frames of Foundation	* Frames Open Comb
	* Supers in place	* Supers added

HEALTH

Signs of Disease: ___ Good Temper: ___

Small Hive Beetle Damage: ___

Nosema Streaking: ___

Signs of Varroa Mite Infestation: ___

Feeding and/or Medication

ACTIONS TAKEN AND NOTES

COLONY CONDITION

Weak: ___ Marginal: ___ Strong: ___

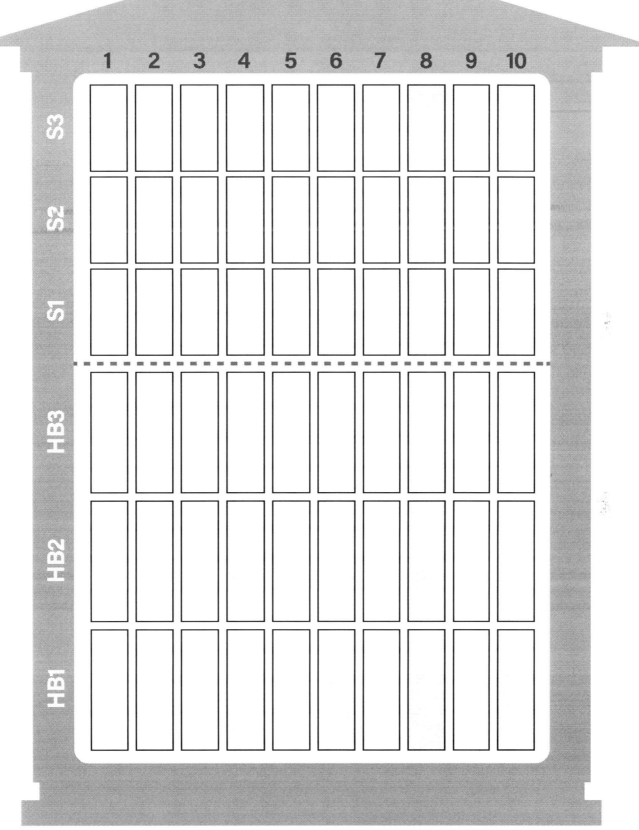

Indicate areas occupied by bees, honey, nectar and pollen. Show the location of vital Queen Cells

HIVE INSPECTION SHEET

Apiary Location:
Hive ID:
Date and Time of Inspection: / / :

INSPECTION DETAILS

Pollen Gathering:
Nectar Flow:
Weather:

Purpose for Inspection

DEVELOPMENT TIMES FOR HONEY BEE

Development (days)	Queen	Worker	Drones
Egg hatches after	3	3	3
Cells Capped after	8	8	10
Adults emerge after	16	21	24

HIVE STATUS

Queen Seen:
Marked:
Eggs:

Queen Cells with Egg, Larva or Pupa	Removed Queen Cells	* Queen Cells Remaining
Emergency	Spotty Drone Brood	* Frames with Brood
Swarm	Worker Brood in All Stages	* Frames of Honey/Nectar
Supersedure	Compact Brood Pattern	* Frames of Pollen
* Frames bees occupy in brood chamber	* Frames of Foundation	* Frames Open Comb
	* Supers in place	* Supers added

HEALTH

Signs of Disease:
Good Temper:
Small Hive Beetle Damage:
Nosema Streaking:
Signs of Varroa Mite Infestation:
Feeding and/or Medication:

ACTIONS TAKEN AND NOTES

COLONY CONDITION

Weak   Marginal   Strong

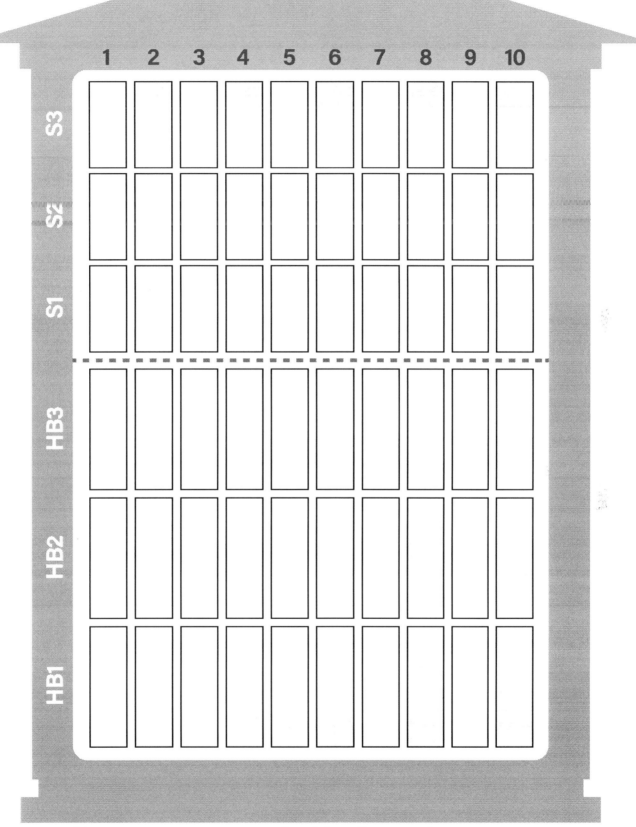

Indicate areas occupied by bees, honey, nectar and pollen. Show the location of vital Queen Cells

HIVE INSPECTION SHEET

Apiary Location		Hive ID	
Date and Time of Inspection	/ / :		

INSPECTION DETAILS

Pollen Gathering		Nectar Flow		Weather	

Purpose for Inspection

DEVELOPMENT TIMES FOR HONEY BEE

Development (days)	Queen	Worker	Drones
Egg hatches after	3	3	3
Cells Capped after	8	8	10
Adults emerge after	16	21	24

HIVE STATUS

Queen Seen		Marked		Eggs	

Queen Cells with Egg, Larva or Pupa		Removed Queen Cells		* Queen Cells Remaining	
		Spotty Drone Brood		* Frames with Brood	
Emergency		Worker Brood in All Stages		* Frames of Honey/Nectar	
Swarm		Compact Brood Pattern		* Frames of Pollen	
Supersedure		* Frames of Foundation		* Frames Open Comb	
* Frames bees occupy in brood chamber		* Supers in place		* Supers added	

HEALTH

Signs of Disease		Good Temper	
Small Hive Beetle Damage			
Nosema Streaking			
Signs of Varroa Mite Infestation			

Feeding and/or Medication

ACTIONS TAKEN AND NOTES

COLONY CONDITION

Weak		Marginal		Strong	

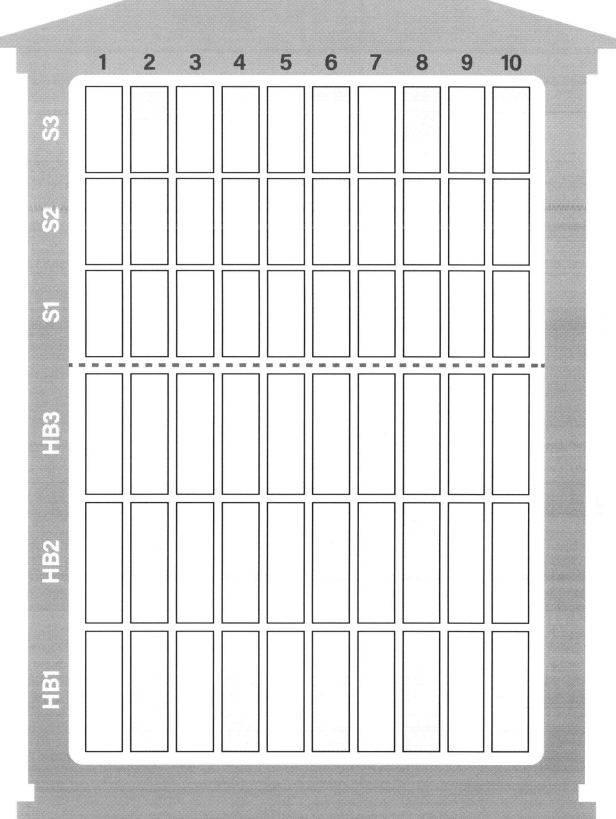

Indicate areas occupied by bees, honey, nectar and pollen. Show the location of vital Queen Cells

HIVE INSPECTION SHEET

Apiary Location: _____
Hive ID: _____
Date and Time of Inspection: __/__/__ : __

INSPECTION DETAILS

Pollen Gathering: ___ **Nectar Flow:** ___ **Weather:** _____

Purpose for Inspection

DEVELOPMENT TIMES FOR HONEY BEE

Development (days)	Queen	Worker	Drones
Egg hatches after	3	3	3
Cells Capped after	8	8	10
Adults emerge after	16	21	24

HIVE STATUS

Queen Seen ___ Marked ___ Eggs ___

- Queen Cells with Egg, Larva or Pupa ___
- Removed Queen Cells ___
- * Queen Cells Remaining ___
- Emergency ___
- Spotty Drone Brood ___
- * Frames with Brood ___
- Swarm ___
- Worker Brood in All Stages ___
- * Frames of Honey/Nectar ___
- Supersedure ___
- Compact Brood Pattern ___
- * Frames of Pollen ___
- * Frames bees occupy in brood chamber ___
- * Frames of Foundation ___
- * Frames Open Comb ___
- * Supers in place ___
- * Supers added ___

HEALTH

- Signs of Disease ___ Good Temper ___
- Small Hive Beetle Damage ___
- Nosema Streaking ___
- Signs of Varroa Mite Infestation ___
- Feeding and/or Medication

ACTIONS TAKEN AND NOTES

COLONY CONDITION

Weak ___ Marginal ___ Strong ___

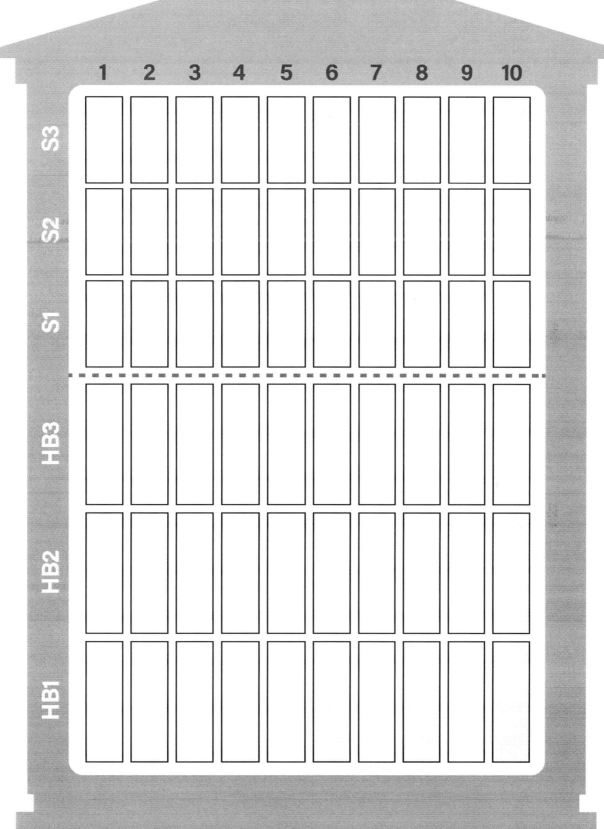

Indicate areas occupied by bees, honey, nectar and pollen. Show the location of vital Queen Cells

HIVE INSPECTION SHEET

Apiary Location: _____   Hive ID: _____

Date and Time of Inspection: __/__/__ :__

INSPECTION DETAILS

Pollen Gathering: ____   Nectar Flow: ____   Weather: _____

Purpose for Inspection

DEVELOPMENT TIMES FOR HONEY BEE

Development (days)	Queen	Worker	Drones
Egg hatches after	3	3	3
Cells Capped after	8	8	10
Adults emerge after	16	21	24

HIVE STATUS

Queen Seen: ____   Marked: ____   Eggs: ____

Queen Cells with Egg, Larva or Pupa	Removed Queen Cells	* Queen Cells Remaining
Emergency	Spotty Drone Brood	* Frames with Brood
Swarm	Worker Brood in All Stages	* Frames of Honey/Nectar
Supersedure	Compact Brood Pattern	* Frames of Pollen
* Frames bees occupy in brood chamber	* Frames of Foundation	* Frames Open Comb
	* Supers in place	* Supers added

HEALTH

Signs of Disease: ____   Good Temper: ____

Small Hive Beetle Damage: ____

Nosema Streaking: ____

Signs of Varroa Mite Infestation: ____

Feeding and/or Medication

ACTIONS TAKEN AND NOTES

COLONY CONDITION

Weak: ____   Marginal: ____   Strong: ____

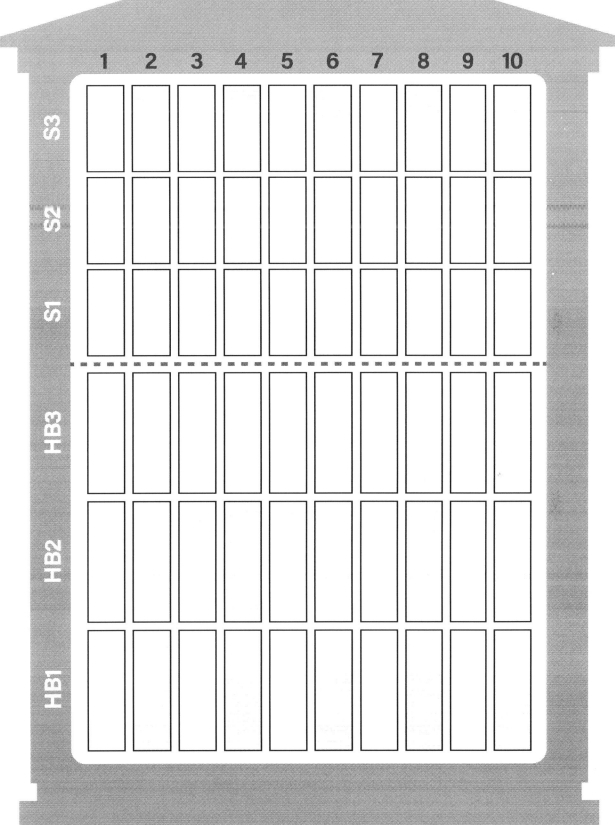

Indicate areas occupied by bees, honey, nectar and pollen. Show the location of vital Queen Cells

HIVE INSPECTION SHEET

Apiary Location: _____

Date and Time of Inspection: __/__/__ __:__

Hive ID: _____

INSPECTION DETAILS

Pollen Gathering: ___ **Nectar Flow:** ___ **Weather:** _____

Purpose for Inspection

DEVELOPMENT TIMES FOR HONEY BEE

Development (days)	Queen	Worker	Drones
Egg hatches after	3	3	3
Cells Capped after	8	8	10
Adults emerge after	16	21	24

HIVE STATUS

Queen Seen: ___ **Marked:** ___ **Eggs:** ___

Queen Cells with Egg, Larva or Pupa	Removed Queen Cells	* Queen Cells Remaining
	Spotty Drone Brood	* Frames with Brood
Emergency	Worker Brood in All Stages	* Frames of Honey/Nectar
Swarm	Compact Brood Pattern	* Frames of Pollen
Supersedure	* Frames of Foundation	* Frames Open Comb
* Frames bees occupy in brood chamber	* Supers in place	* Supers added

HEALTH

Signs of Disease: ___ **Good Temper:** ___

Small Hive Beetle Damage: ___

Nosema Streaking: ___

Signs of Varroa Mite Infestation: ___

Feeding and/or Medication

ACTIONS TAKEN AND NOTES

COLONY CONDITION

Weak: ___ **Marginal:** ___ **Strong:** ___

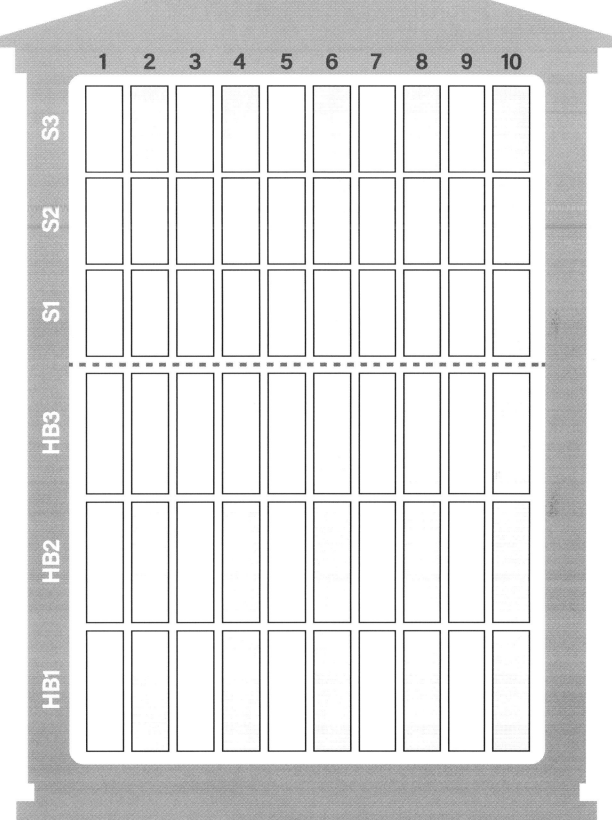

Indicate areas occupied by bees, honey, nectar and pollen. Show the location of vital Queen Cells

HIVE INSPECTION SHEET

Apiary Location: _____
Hive ID: _____
Date and Time of Inspection: __/__/__ :

INSPECTION DETAILS

Pollen Gathering: ____ **Nectar Flow:** ____ **Weather:** ____

Purpose for Inspection

DEVELOPMENT TIMES FOR HONEY BEE

Development (days)	Queen	Worker	Drones
Egg hatches after	3	3	3
Cells Capped after	8	8	10
Adults emerge after	16	21	24

HIVE STATUS

Queen Seen: ____ **Marked:** ____ **Eggs:** ____

Queen Cells with Egg, Larva or Pupa	Removed Queen Cells	* Queen Cells Remaining
Emergency	Spotty Drone Brood	* Frames with Brood
Swarm	Worker Brood in All Stages	* Frames of Honey/Nectar
Supersedure	Compact Brood Pattern	* Frames of Pollen
* Frames bees occupy in brood chamber	* Frames of Foundation	* Frames Open Comb
	* Supers in place	* Supers added

HEALTH

Signs of Disease: ____ **Good Temper:** ____
Small Hive Beetle Damage: ____
Nosema Streaking: ____
Signs of Varroa Mite Infestation: ____

Feeding and/or Medication

ACTIONS TAKEN AND NOTES

COLONY CONDITION

Weak: ____ **Marginal:** ____ **Strong:** ____

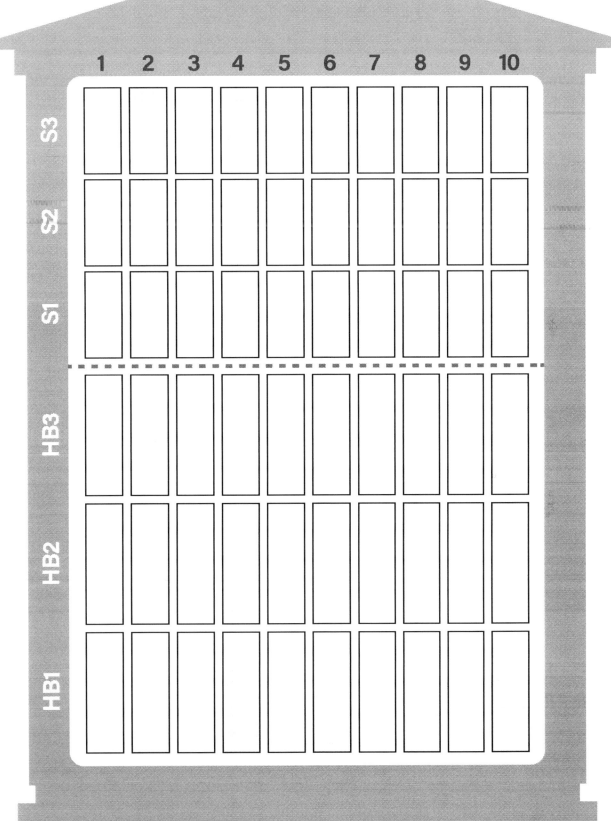

Indicate areas occupied by bees, honey, nectar and pollen. Show the location of vital Queen Cells

HIVE INSPECTION SHEET

Apiary Location: _____
Hive ID: _____
Date and Time of Inspection: __/__/__ __:__

INSPECTION DETAILS

Pollen Gathering: ____   Nectar Flow: ____   Weather: _____

Purpose for Inspection

DEVELOPMENT TIMES FOR HONEY BEE

Development (days)	Queen	Worker	Drones
Egg hatches after	3	3	3
Cells Capped after	8	8	10
Adults emerge after	16	21	24

HIVE STATUS

Queen Seen: ____   Marked: ____   Eggs: ____

Queen Cells with Egg, Larva or Pupa	Removed Queen Cells	* Queen Cells Remaining
	Spotty Drone Brood	* Frames with Brood
Emergency	Worker Brood in All Stages	* Frames of Honey/Nectar
Swarm	Compact Brood Pattern	* Frames of Pollen
Supersedure	* Frames of Foundation	* Frames Open Comb
* Frames bees occupy in brood chamber	* Supers in place	* Supers added

HEALTH

Signs of Disease: ____   Good Temper: ____
Small Hive Beetle Damage: ____
Nosema Streaking: ____
Signs of Varroa Mite Infestation: ____

Feeding and/or Medication

ACTIONS TAKEN AND NOTES

COLONY CONDITION

Weak: ____   Marginal: ____   Strong: ____

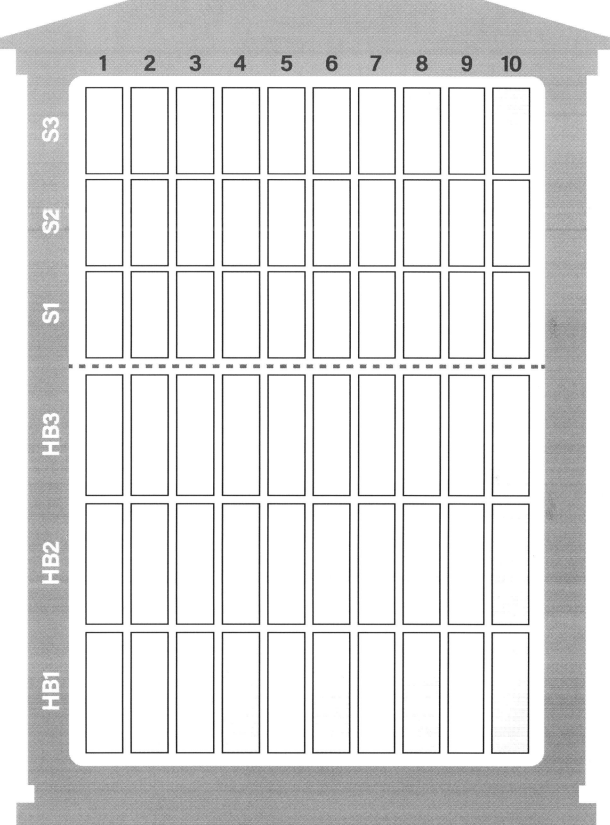

Indicate areas occupied by bees, honey, nectar and pollen. Show the location of vital Queen Cells

HIVE INSPECTION SHEET

Apiary Location: _____
Hive ID: _____
Date and Time of Inspection: ___/___/___ ___:___

INSPECTION DETAILS

Pollen Gathering: ____ **Nectar Flow:** ____ **Weather:** _____

Purpose for Inspection

_____

DEVELOPMENT TIMES FOR HONEY BEE

Development (days)	Queen	Worker	Drones
Egg hatches after	3	3	3
Cells Capped after	8	8	10
Adults emerge after	16	21	24

HIVE STATUS

Queen Seen: ____ **Marked:** ____ **Eggs:** ____

Queen Cells with Egg, Larva or Pupa	Removed Queen Cells	* Queen Cells Remaining
Emergency	Spotty Drone Brood	* Frames with Brood
Swarm	Worker Brood in All Stages	* Frames of Honey/Nectar
Supersedure	Compact Brood Pattern	* Frames of Pollen
* Frames bees occupy in brood chamber	* Frames of Foundation	* Frames Open Comb
	* Supers in place	* Supers added

HEALTH

Signs of Disease: ____ **Good Temper:** ____
Small Hive Beetle Damage: ____
Nosema Streaking: ____
Signs of Varroa Mite Infestation: ____

Feeding and/or Medication

_____

ACTIONS TAKEN AND NOTES

_____

COLONY CONDITION

Weak: ____ **Marginal:** ____ **Strong:** ____

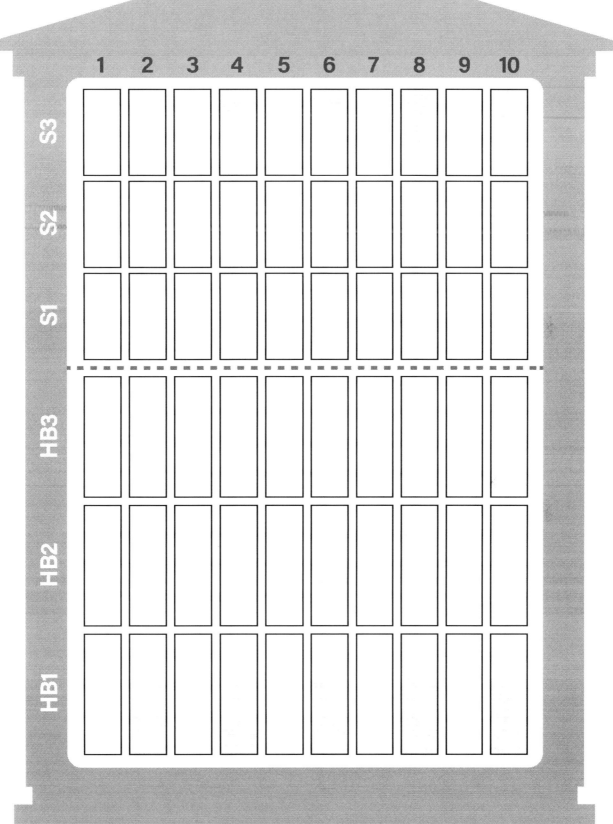

Indicate areas occupied by bees, honey, nectar and pollen. Show the location of vital Queen Cells

HIVE INSPECTION SHEET

Apiary Location: _____
Hive ID: _____
Date and Time of Inspection: __/__/__ __:__

INSPECTION DETAILS

Pollen Gathering: ____ Nectar Flow: ____ Weather: _____

Purpose for Inspection

_____

DEVELOPMENT TIMES FOR HONEY BEE

Development (days)	Queen	Worker	Drones
Egg hatches after	3	3	3
Cells Capped after	8	8	10
Adults emerge after	16	21	24

HIVE STATUS

Queen Seen: ____ Marked: ____ Eggs: ____

Queen Cells with Egg, Larva or Pupa	Removed Queen Cells	* Queen Cells Remaining
Emergency	Spotty Drone Brood	* Frames with Brood
Swarm	Worker Brood in All Stages	* Frames of Honey/Nectar
Supersedure	Compact Brood Pattern	* Frames of Pollen
* Frames bees occupy in brood chamber	* Frames of Foundation	* Frames Open Comb
	* Supers in place	* Supers added

HEALTH

Signs of Disease: ____ Good Temper: ____
Small Hive Beetle Damage: ____
Nosema Streaking: ____
Signs of Varroa Mite Infestation: ____

Feeding and/or Medication:
_____

ACTIONS TAKEN AND NOTES

_____

COLONY CONDITION

Weak: ____ Marginal: ____ Strong: ____

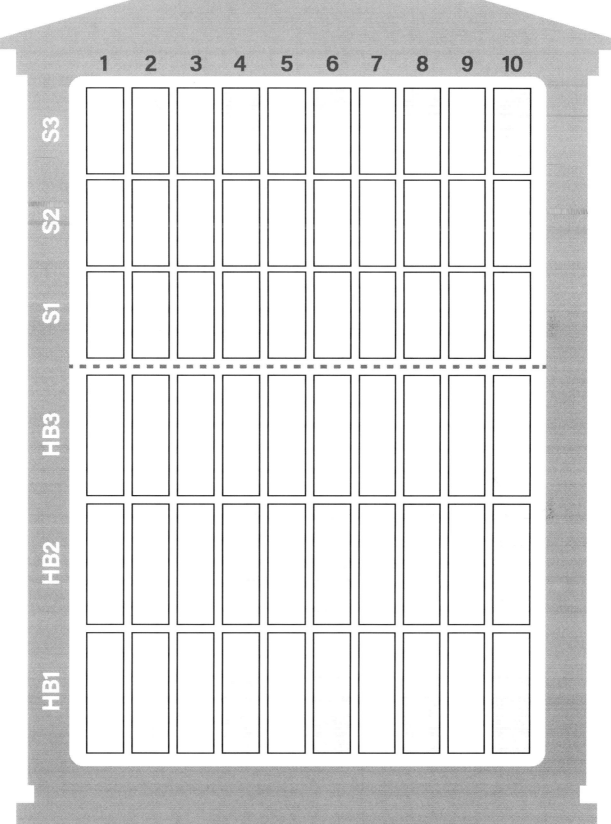

Indicate areas occupied by bees, honey, nectar and pollen. Show the location of vital Queen Cells

HIVE INSPECTION SHEET

Apiary Location:
Hive ID:
Date and Time of Inspection: / / :

INSPECTION DETAILS

Pollen Gathering:
Nectar Flow:
Weather:

Purpose for Inspection

DEVELOPMENT TIMES FOR HONEY BEE

Development (days)	Queen	Worker	Drones
Egg hatches after	3	3	3
Cells Capped after	8	8	10
Adults emerge after	16	21	24

HIVE STATUS

Queen Seen:
Marked:
Eggs:

- Queen Cells with Egg, Larva or Pupa:
- Removed Queen Cells:
- * Queen Cells Remaining:
- Emergency:
- Spotty Drone Brood:
- * Frames with Brood:
- Swarm:
- Worker Brood in All Stages:
- * Frames of Honey/Nectar:
- Supersedure:
- Compact Brood Pattern:
- * Frames of Pollen:
- * Frames bees occupy in brood chamber:
- * Frames of Foundation:
- * Frames Open Comb:
- * Supers in place:
- * Supers added:

HEALTH

- Signs of Disease:
- Good Temper:
- Small Hive Beetle Damage:
- Nosema Streaking:
- Signs of Varroa Mite Infestation:
- Feeding and/or Medication:

ACTIONS TAKEN AND NOTES

COLONY CONDITION

Weak:
Marginal:
Strong:

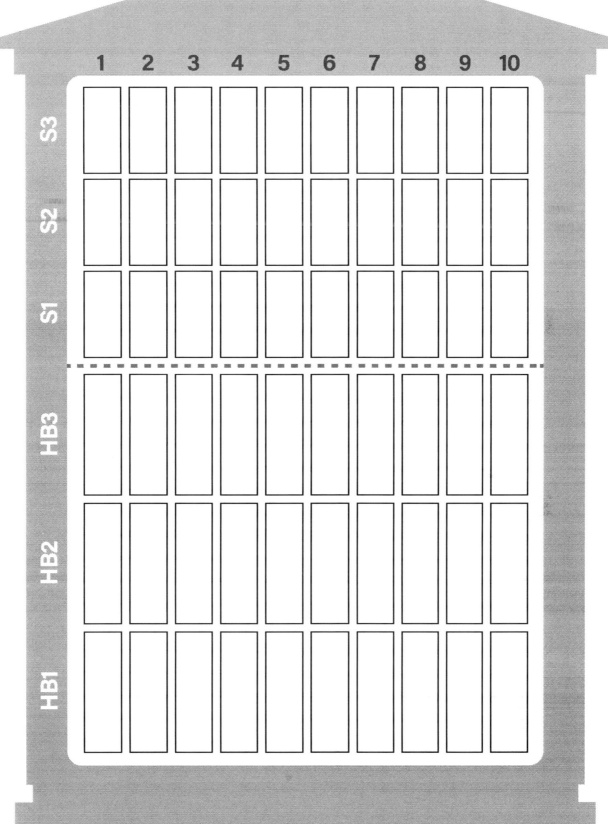

Indicate areas occupied by bees, honey, nectar and pollen. Show the location of vital Queen Cells

HIVE INSPECTION SHEET

Apiary Location: _____
Hive ID: _____
Date and Time of Inspection: ___/___/___ ___:___

INSPECTION DETAILS

Pollen Gathering: ___   Nectar Flow: ___   Weather: _____

Purpose for Inspection

DEVELOPMENT TIMES FOR HONEY BEE

Development (days)	Queen	Worker	Drones
Egg hatches after	3	3	3
Cells Capped after	8	8	10
Adults emerge after	16	21	24

HIVE STATUS

Queen Seen: ___   Marked: ___   Eggs: ___

Queen Cells with Egg, Larva or Pupa	Removed Queen Cells	* Queen Cells Remaining
Emergency	Spotty Drone Brood	* Frames with Brood
Swarm	Worker Brood in All Stages	* Frames of Honey/Nectar
Supersedure	Compact Brood Pattern	* Frames of Pollen
* Frames bees occupy in brood chamber	* Frames of Foundation	* Frames Open Comb
	* Supers in place	* Supers added

HEALTH

Signs of Disease: ___   Good Temper: ___
Small Hive Beetle Damage: ___
Nosema Streaking: ___
Signs of Varroa Mite Infestation: ___

Feeding and/or Medication: _____

ACTIONS TAKEN AND NOTES

COLONY CONDITION

Weak: ___   Marginal: ___   Strong: ___

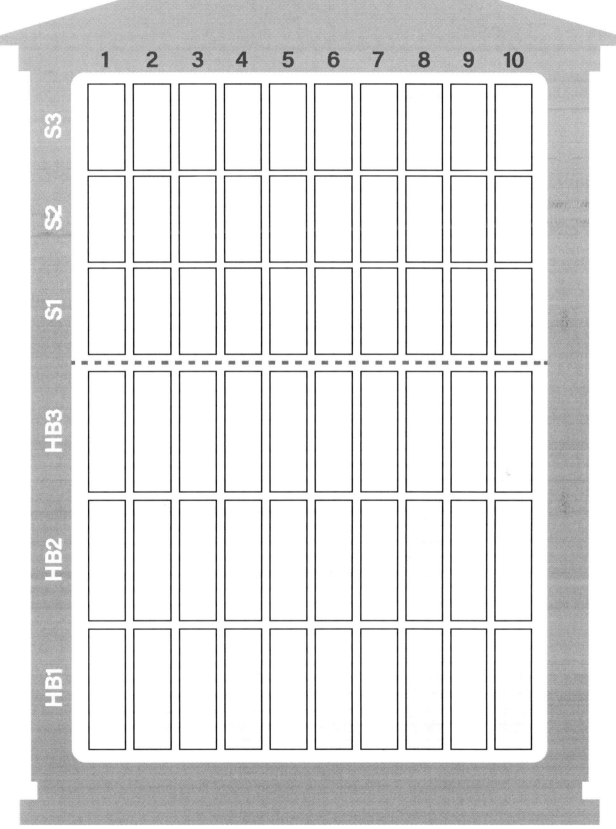

Indicate areas occupied by bees, honey, nectar and pollen. Show the location of vital Queen Cells

HIVE INSPECTION SHEET

Apiary Location		Hive ID	
Date and Time of Inspection	/ / :		

INSPECTION DETAILS

Pollen Gathering		Nectar Flow		Weather	

Purpose for Inspection

DEVELOPMENT TIMES FOR HONEY BEE

Development (days)	Queen	Worker	Drones
Egg hatches after	3	3	3
Cells Capped after	8	8	10
Adults emerge after	16	21	24

HIVE STATUS

Queen Seen		Marked		Eggs	

Queen Cells with Egg, Larva or Pupa		Removed Queen Cells		* Queen Cells Remaining	
		Spotty Drone Brood		* Frames with Brood	
Emergency		Worker Brood in All Stages		* Frames of Honey/Nectar	
Swarm		Compact Brood Pattern		* Frames of Pollen	
Supersedure		* Frames of Foundation		* Frames Open Comb	
* Frames bees occupy in brood chamber		* Supers in place		* Supers added	

HEALTH

Signs of Disease		Good Temper	
Small Hive Beetle Damage			
Nosema Streaking			
Signs of Varroa Mite Infestation			
Feeding and/or Medication			

ACTIONS TAKEN AND NOTES

COLONY CONDITION

Weak		Marginal		Strong	

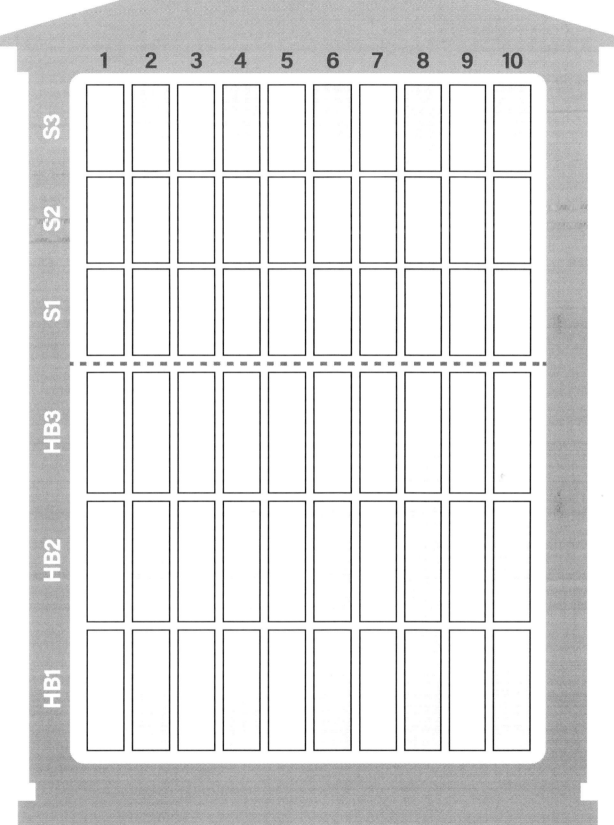

Indicate areas occupied by bees, honey, nectar and pollen. Show the location of vital Queen Cells

HIVE INSPECTION SHEET

Apiary Location		Hive ID	
Date and Time of Inspection	/ / :		

INSPECTION DETAILS

| Pollen Gathering | | Nectar Flow | | Weather | |

Purpose for Inspection

DEVELOPMENT TIMES FOR HONEY BEE

Development (days)	Queen	Worker	Drones
Egg hatches after	3	3	3
Cells Capped after	8	8	10
Adults emerge after	16	21	24

HIVE STATUS

| Queen Seen | | Marked | | Eggs | |

Queen Cells with Egg, Larva or Pupa		Removed Queen Cells		* Queen Cells Remaining	
		Spotty Drone Brood		* Frames with Brood	
Emergency		Worker Brood in All Stages		* Frames of Honey/Nectar	
Swarm		Compact Brood Pattern		* Frames of Pollen	
Supersedure		* Frames of Foundation		* Frames Open Comb	
* Frames bees occupy in brood chamber		* Supers in place		* Supers added	

HEALTH

Signs of Disease		Good Temper	
Small Hive Beetle Damage			
Nosema Streaking			
Signs of Varroa Mite Infestation			

Feeding and/or Medication

ACTIONS TAKEN AND NOTES

COLONY CONDITION

| Weak | | Marginal | | Strong | |

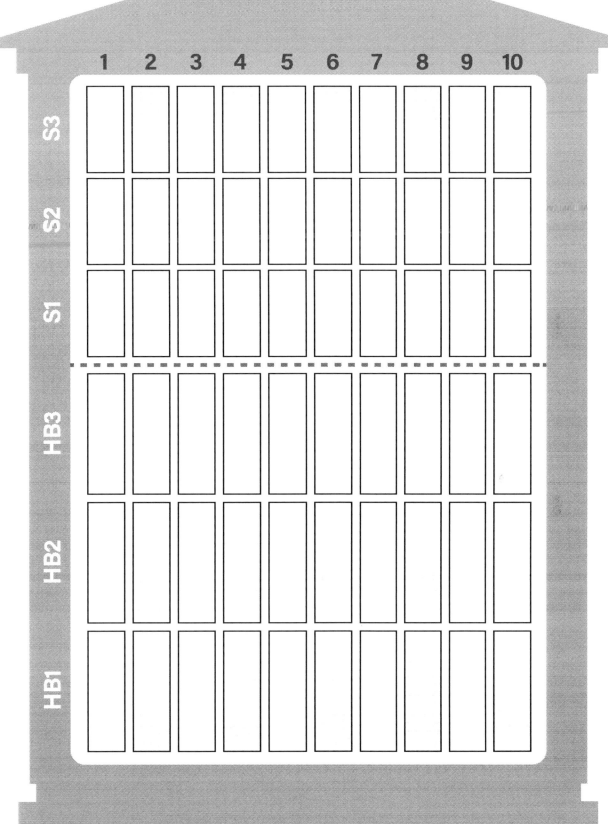

Indicate areas occupied by bees, honey, nectar and pollen. Show the location of vital Queen Cells

HIVE INSPECTION SHEET

Apiary Location: _____
Date and Time of Inspection: __/__/__ __:__
Hive ID: _____

INSPECTION DETAILS

Pollen Gathering: ____ **Nectar Flow:** ____ **Weather:** ____

Purpose for Inspection

DEVELOPMENT TIMES FOR HONEY BEE

Development (days)	Queen	Worker	Drones
Egg hatches after	3	3	3
Cells Capped after	8	8	10
Adults emerge after	16	21	24

HIVE STATUS

Queen Seen: ____ **Marked:** ____ **Eggs:** ____

Queen Cells with Egg, Larva or Pupa	Removed Queen Cells	* Queen Cells Remaining
	Spotty Drone Brood	* Frames with Brood
Emergency	Worker Brood in All Stages	* Frames of Honey/Nectar
Swarm	Compact Brood Pattern	* Frames of Pollen
Supersedure	* Frames of Foundation	* Frames Open Comb
* Frames bees occupy in brood chamber	* Supers in place	* Supers added

HEALTH

Signs of Disease: ____ **Good Temper:** ____
Small Hive Beetle Damage: ____
Nosema Streaking: ____
Signs of Varroa Mite Infestation: ____
Feeding and/or Medication:

ACTIONS TAKEN AND NOTES

COLONY CONDITION

Weak: ____ **Marginal:** ____ **Strong:** ____

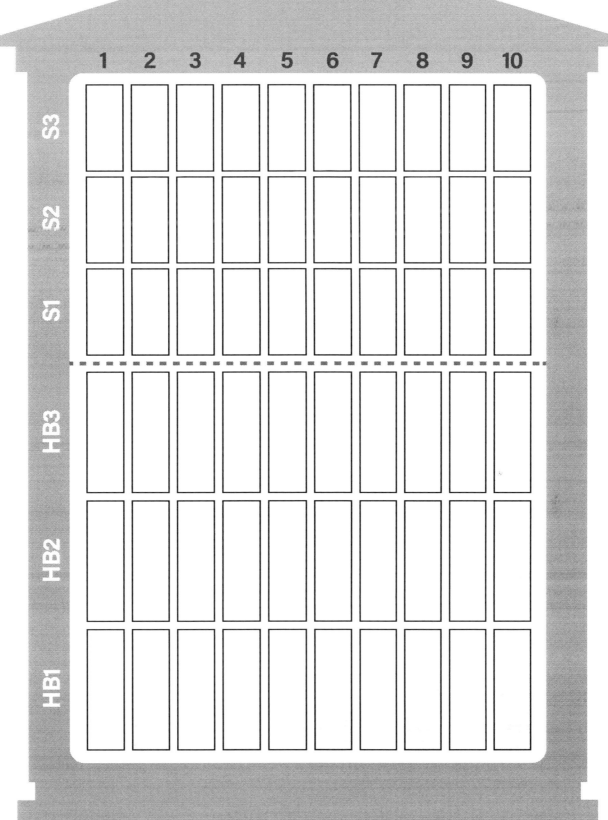

Indicate areas occupied by bees, honey, nectar and pollen. Show the location of vital Queen Cells

HIVE INSPECTION SHEET

Apiary Location: _____ Hive ID: _____

Date and Time of Inspection: __/__/__ : __

INSPECTION DETAILS

Pollen Gathering: ____ Nectar Flow: ____ Weather: _____

Purpose for Inspection

DEVELOPMENT TIMES FOR HONEY BEE

Development (days)	Queen	Worker	Drones
Egg hatches after	3	3	3
Cells Capped after	8	8	10
Adults emerge after	16	21	24

HIVE STATUS

Queen Seen: ____ Marked: ____ Eggs: ____

Queen Cells with Egg, Larva or Pupa	Removed Queen Cells	* Queen Cells Remaining
	Spotty Drone Brood	* Frames with Brood
Emergency	Worker Brood in All Stages	* Frames of Honey/Nectar
Swarm	Compact Brood Pattern	* Frames of Pollen
Supersedure	* Frames of Foundation	* Frames Open Comb
* Frames bees occupy in brood chamber	* Supers in place	* Supers added

HEALTH

Signs of Disease: ____ Good Temper: ____

Small Hive Beetle Damage: ____

Nosema Streaking: ____

Signs of Varroa Mite Infestation: ____

Feeding and/or Medication: ____

ACTIONS TAKEN AND NOTES

COLONY CONDITION

Weak: ____ Marginal: ____ Strong: ____

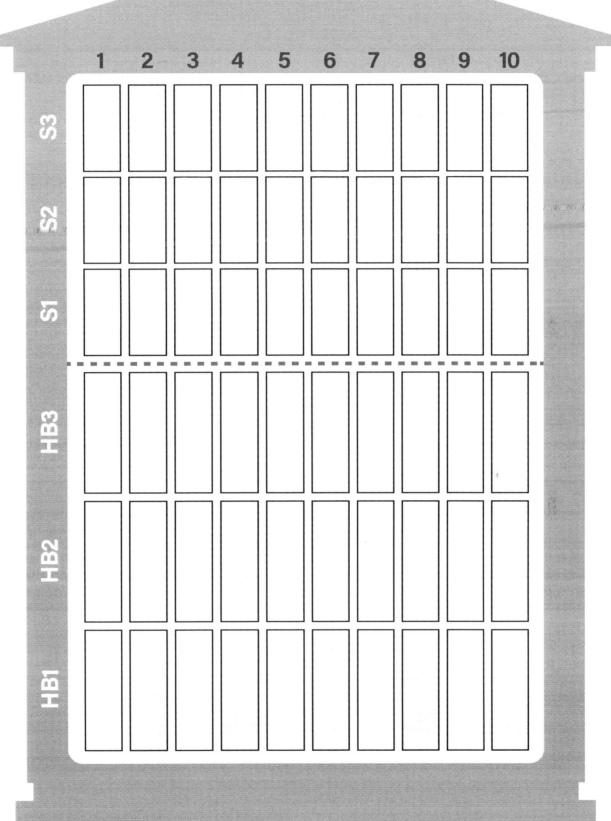

Indicate areas occupied by bees, honey, nectar and pollen. Show the location of vital Queen Cells

HIVE INSPECTION SHEET

Apiary Location		Hive ID	
Date and Time of Inspection	/ / :		

INSPECTION DETAILS

Pollen Gathering		Nectar Flow		Weather	

Purpose for Inspection

DEVELOPMENT TIMES FOR HONEY BEE

Development (days)	Queen	Worker	Drones
Egg hatches after	3	3	3
Cells Capped after	8	8	10
Adults emerge after	16	21	24

HIVE STATUS

Queen Seen		Marked		Eggs	

Queen Cells with Egg, Larva or Pupa		Removed Queen Cells		* Queen Cells Remaining	
		Spotty Drone Brood		* Frames with Brood	
Emergency		Worker Brood in All Stages		* Frames of Honey/Nectar	
Swarm		Compact Brood Pattern		* Frames of Pollen	
Supersedure		* Frames of Foundation		* Frames Open Comb	
* Frames bees occupy in brood chamber		* Supers in place		* Supers added	

HEALTH

Signs of Disease		Good Temper	
Small Hive Beetle Damage			
Nosema Streaking			
Signs of Varroa Mite Infestation			
Feeding and/or Medication			

ACTIONS TAKEN AND NOTES

COLONY CONDITION

Weak		Marginal		Strong	

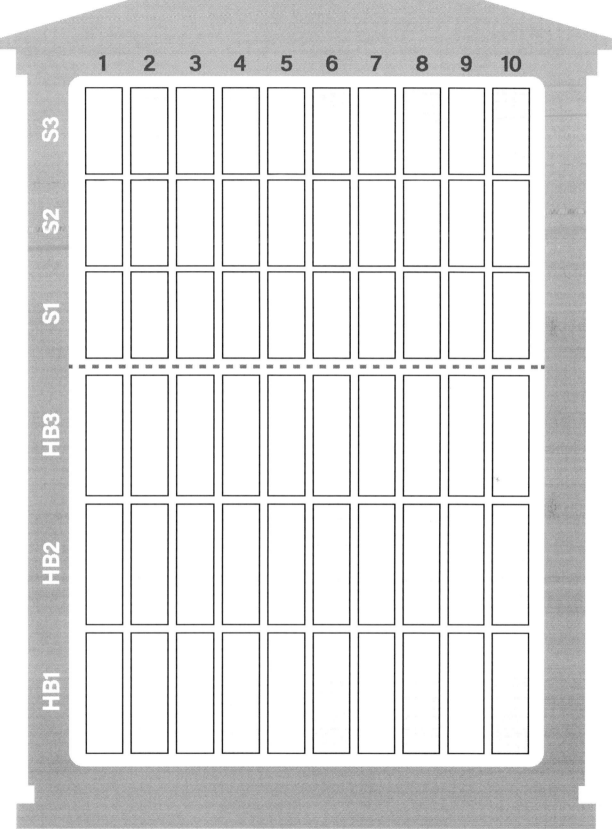

Indicate areas occupied by bees, honey, nectar and pollen. Show the location of vital Queen Cells

HIVE INSPECTION SHEET

Apiary Location:
Hive ID:
Date and Time of Inspection: / / :

INSPECTION DETAILS

Pollen Gathering: **Nectar Flow:** **Weather:**

Purpose for Inspection

DEVELOPMENT TIMES FOR HONEY BEE

Development (days)	Queen	Worker	Drones
Egg hatches after	3	3	3
Cells Capped after	8	8	10
Adults emerge after	16	21	24

HIVE STATUS

Queen Seen: Marked: Eggs:

Queen Cells with Egg, Larva or Pupa	Removed Queen Cells	* Queen Cells Remaining
	Spotty Drone Brood	* Frames with Brood
Emergency	Worker Brood in All Stages	* Frames of Honey/Nectar
Swarm	Compact Brood Pattern	* Frames of Pollen
Supersedure	* Frames of Foundation	* Frames Open Comb
* Frames bees occupy in brood chamber	* Supers in place	* Supers added

HEALTH

Signs of Disease: Good Temper:
Small Hive Beetle Damage:
Nosema Streaking:
Signs of Varroa Mite Infestation:
Feeding and/or Medication:

ACTIONS TAKEN AND NOTES

COLONY CONDITION

Weak: Marginal: Strong:

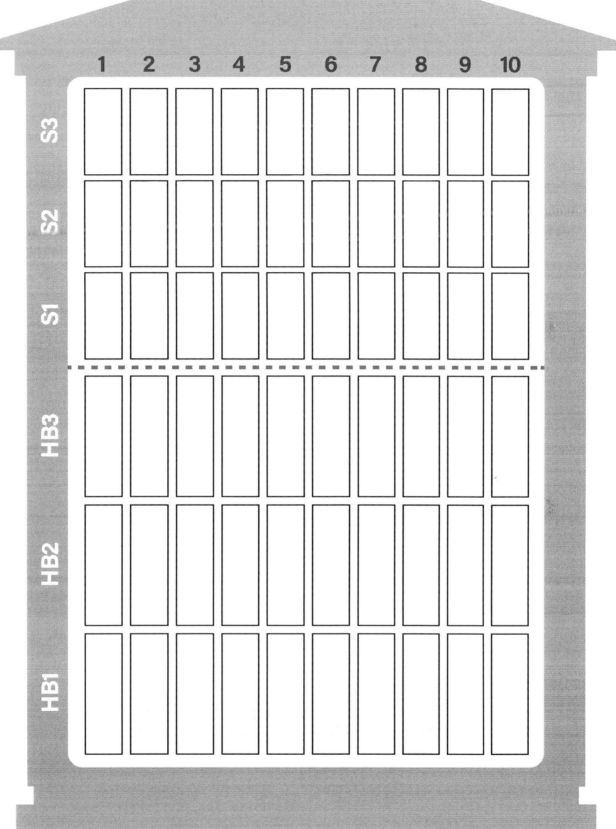

Indicate areas occupied by bees, honey, nectar and pollen. Show the location of vital Queen Cells

HIVE INSPECTION SHEET

Apiary Location:
Hive ID:
Date and Time of Inspection: / / :

INSPECTION DETAILS

Pollen Gathering: **Nectar Flow:** **Weather:**

Purpose for Inspection

DEVELOPMENT TIMES FOR HONEY BEE

Development (days)	Queen	Worker	Drones
Egg hatches after	3	3	3
Cells Capped after	8	8	10
Adults emerge after	16	21	24

HIVE STATUS

Queen Seen: **Marked:** **Eggs:**

Queen Cells with Egg, Larva or Pupa	Removed Queen Cells	* Queen Cells Remaining
Emergency	Spotty Drone Brood	* Frames with Brood
Swarm	Worker Brood in All Stages	* Frames of Honey/Nectar
Supersedure	Compact Brood Pattern	* Frames of Pollen
* Frames bees occupy in brood chamber	* Frames of Foundation	* Frames Open Comb
	* Supers in place	* Supers added

HEALTH

Signs of Disease: **Good Temper:**
Small Hive Beetle Damage:
Nosema Streaking:
Signs of Varroa Mite Infestation:
Feeding and/or Medication:

ACTIONS TAKEN AND NOTES

COLONY CONDITION

Weak **Marginal** **Strong**

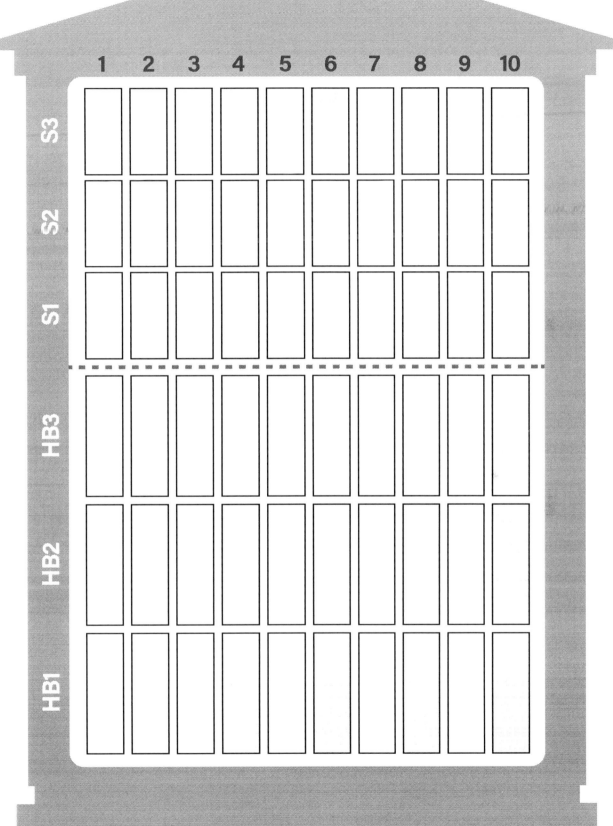

Indicate areas occupied by bees, honey, nectar and pollen. Show the location of vital Queen Cells

HIVE INSPECTION SHEET

Apiary Location:
Hive ID:
Date and Time of Inspection: / / :

INSPECTION DETAILS

Pollen Gathering:
Nectar Flow:
Weather:

Purpose for Inspection

DEVELOPMENT TIMES FOR HONEY BEE

Development (days)	Queen	Worker	Drones
Egg hatches after	3	3	3
Cells Capped after	8	8	10
Adults emerge after	16	21	24

HIVE STATUS

Queen Seen:
Marked:
Eggs:

Queen Cells with Egg, Larva or Pupa	Removed Queen Cells	* Queen Cells Remaining
	Spotty Drone Brood	* Frames with Brood
Emergency	Worker Brood in All Stages	* Frames of Honey/Nectar
Swarm	Compact Brood Pattern	* Frames of Pollen
Supersedure	* Frames of Foundation	* Frames Open Comb
* Frames bees occupy in brood chamber	* Supers in place	* Supers added

HEALTH

Signs of Disease:
Good Temper:
Small Hive Beetle Damage:
Nosema Streaking:
Signs of Varroa Mite Infestation:
Feeding and/or Medication:

ACTIONS TAKEN AND NOTES

COLONY CONDITION

Weak Marginal Strong

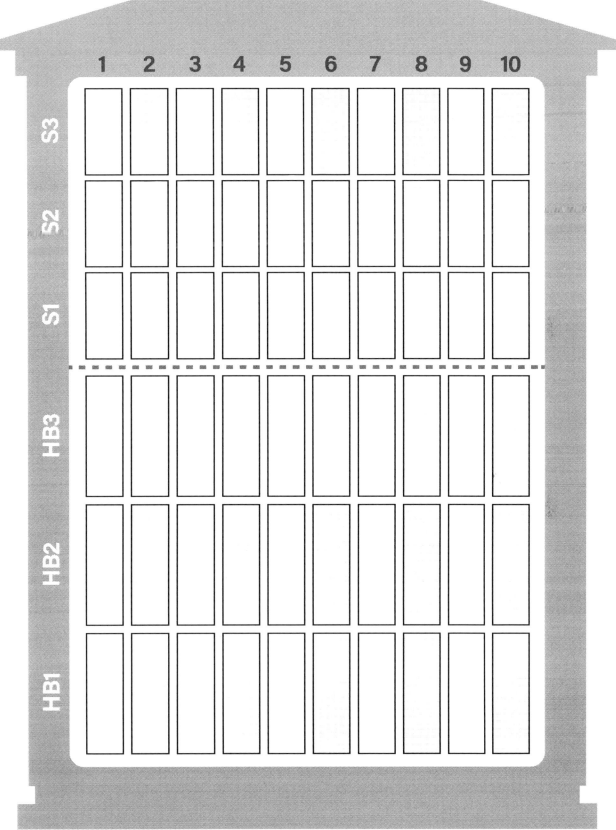

Indicate areas occupied by bees, honey, nectar and pollen. Show the location of vital Queen Cells

HIVE INSPECTION SHEET

Apiary Location		Hive ID	
Date and Time of Inspection	/ / :		

INSPECTION DETAILS

Pollen Gathering		Nectar Flow		Weather	

Purpose for Inspection

DEVELOPMENT TIMES FOR HONEY BEE

Development (days)	Queen	Worker	Drones
Egg hatches after	3	3	3
Cells Capped after	8	8	10
Adults emerge after	16	21	24

HIVE STATUS

Queen Seen		Marked		Eggs	

Queen Cells with Egg, Larva or Pupa		Removed Queen Cells		* Queen Cells Remaining	
Emergency		Spotty Drone Brood		* Frames with Brood	
Swarm		Worker Brood in All Stages		* Frames of Honey/Nectar	
Supersedure		Compact Brood Pattern		* Frames of Pollen	
* Frames bees occupy in brood chamber		* Frames of Foundation		* Frames Open Comb	
		* Supers in place		* Supers added	

HEALTH

Signs of Disease		Good Temper	
Small Hive Beetle Damage			
Nosema Streaking			
Signs of Varroa Mite Infestation			

Feeding and/or Medication

ACTIONS TAKEN AND NOTES

COLONY CONDITION

Weak		Marginal		Strong	

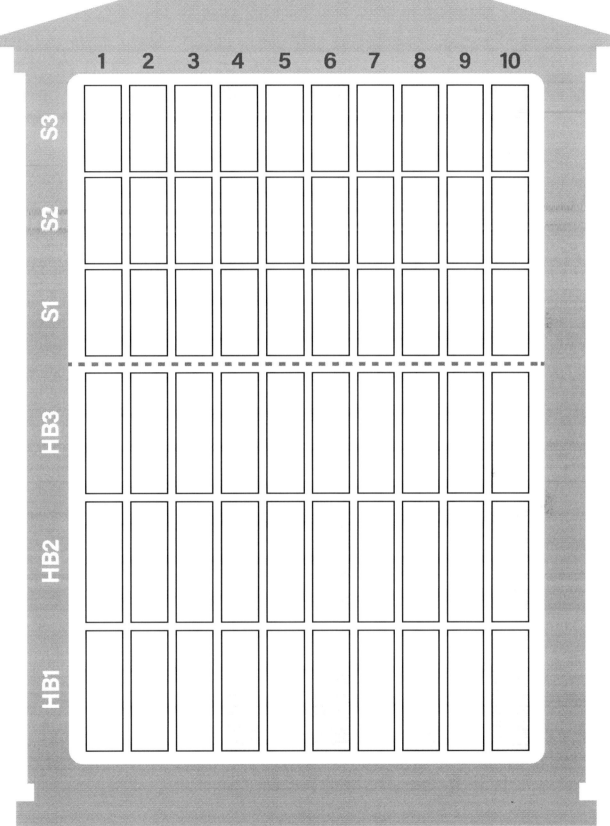

Indicate areas occupied by bees, honey, nectar and pollen. Show the location of vital Queen Cells

HIVE INSPECTION SHEET

Apiary Location		Hive ID	
Date and Time of Inspection	/ / :		

INSPECTION DETAILS

Pollen Gathering		Nectar Flow		Weather	

Purpose for Inspection

DEVELOPMENT TIMES FOR HONEY BEE

Development (days)	Queen	Worker	Drones
Egg hatches after	3	3	3
Cells Capped after	8	8	10
Adults emerge after	16	21	24

HIVE STATUS

Queen Seen		Marked		Eggs	

Queen Cells with Egg, Larva or Pupa		Removed Queen Cells		* Queen Cells Remaining	
		Spotty Drone Brood		* Frames with Brood	
Emergency		Worker Brood in All Stages		* Frames of Honey/Nectar	
Swarm		Compact Brood Pattern		* Frames of Pollen	
Supersedure		* Frames of Foundation		* Frames Open Comb	
* Frames bees occupy in brood chamber		* Supers in place		* Supers added	

HEALTH

Signs of Disease		Good Temper	
Small Hive Beetle Damage			
Nosema Streaking			
Signs of Varroa Mite Infestation			
Feeding and/or Medication			

ACTIONS TAKEN AND NOTES

COLONY CONDITION

Weak		Marginal		Strong	

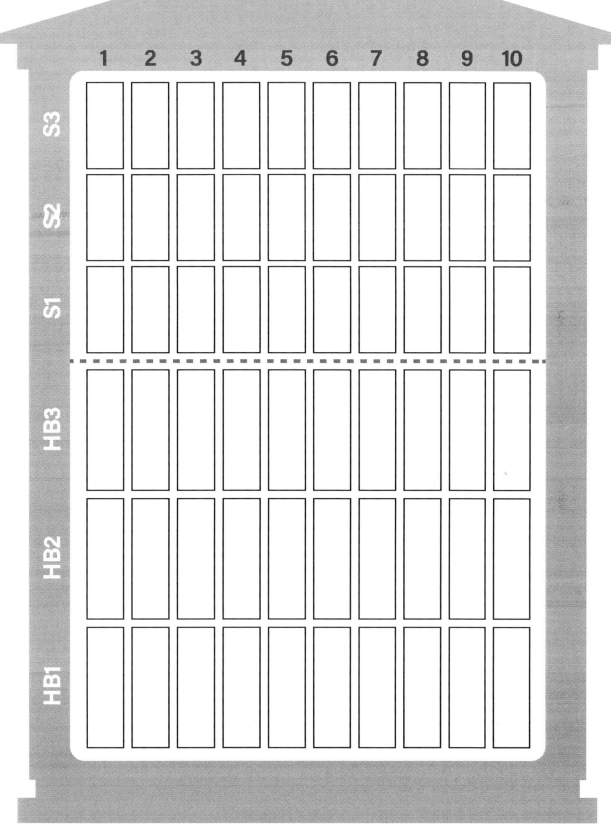

Indicate areas occupied by bees, honey, nectar and pollen. Show the location of vital Queen Cells

HIVE INSPECTION SHEET

Apiary Location: _____
Hive ID: _____
Date and Time of Inspection: ___/___/___ ___:___

INSPECTION DETAILS

Pollen Gathering: ___   **Nectar Flow:** ___   **Weather:** _____

Purpose for Inspection

DEVELOPMENT TIMES FOR HONEY BEE

Development (days)	Queen	Worker	Drones
Egg hatches after	3	3	3
Cells Capped after	8	8	10
Adults emerge after	16	21	24

HIVE STATUS

Queen Seen ___   Marked ___   Eggs ___

Queen Cells with Egg, Larva or Pupa	Removed Queen Cells	* Queen Cells Remaining
	Spotty Drone Brood	* Frames with Brood
Emergency	Worker Brood in All Stages	* Frames of Honey/Nectar
Swarm	Compact Brood Pattern	* Frames of Pollen
Supersedure	* Frames of Foundation	* Frames Open Comb
* Frames bees occupy in brood chamber	* Supers in place	* Supers added

HEALTH

Signs of Disease ___   Good Temper ___
Small Hive Beetle Damage ___
Nosema Streaking ___
Signs of Varroa Mite Infestation ___
Feeding and/or Medication

ACTIONS TAKEN AND NOTES

COLONY CONDITION

Weak ___   Marginal ___   Strong ___

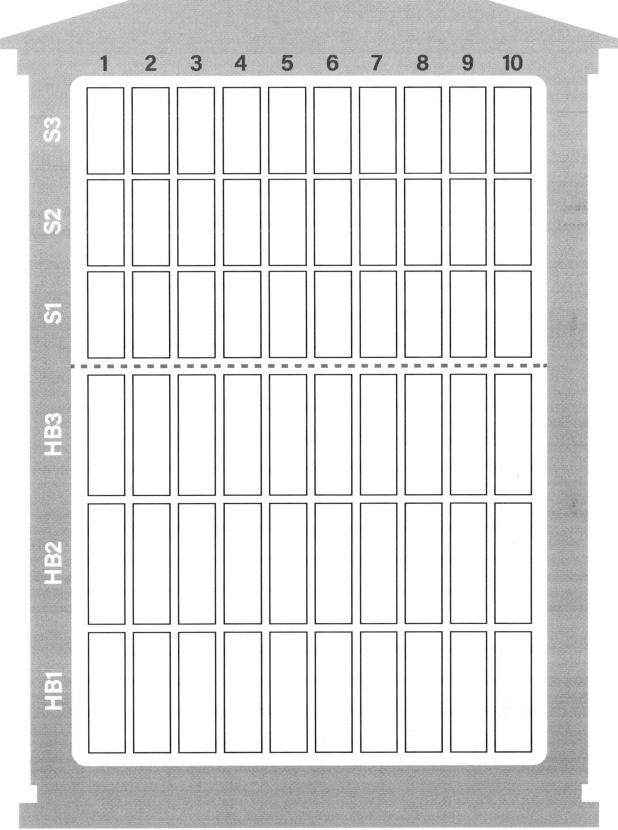

Indicate areas occupied by bees, honey, nectar and pollen. Show the location of vital Queen Cells

HIVE INSPECTION SHEET

Apiary Location: _____ Hive ID: _____

Date and Time of Inspection: __/__/__ :

INSPECTION DETAILS

Pollen Gathering: ____   Nectar Flow: ____   Weather: _____

Purpose for Inspection

DEVELOPMENT TIMES FOR HONEY BEE

Development (days)	Queen	Worker	Drones
Egg hatches after	3	3	3
Cells Capped after	8	8	10
Adults emerge after	16	21	24

HIVE STATUS

Queen Seen: ____   Marked: ____   Eggs: ____

Queen Cells with Egg, Larva or Pupa	Removed Queen Cells	* Queen Cells Remaining
	Spotty Drone Brood	* Frames with Brood
Emergency	Worker Brood in All Stages	* Frames of Honey/Nectar
Swarm	Compact Brood Pattern	* Frames of Pollen
Supersedure	* Frames of Foundation	* Frames Open Comb
* Frames bees occupy in brood chamber	* Supers in place	* Supers added

HEALTH

Signs of Disease: ____   Good Temper: ____

Small Hive Beetle Damage: ____

Nosema Streaking: ____

Signs of Varroa Mite Infestation: ____

Feeding and/or Medication:

ACTIONS TAKEN AND NOTES

COLONY CONDITION

Weak: ____   Marginal: ____   Strong: ____

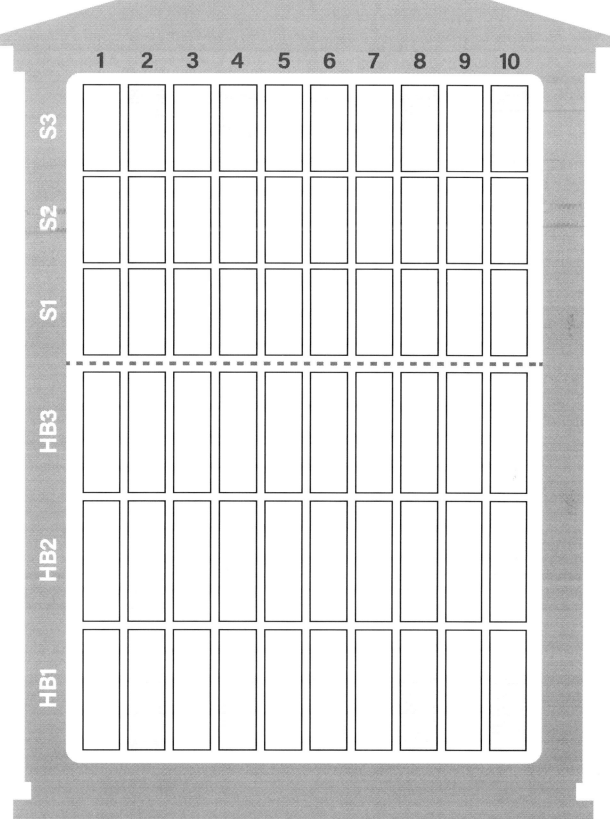

Indicate areas occupied by bees, honey, nectar and pollen. Show the location of vital Queen Cells

HIVE INSPECTION SHEET

Apiary Location		Hive ID	
Date and Time of Inspection	/ / :		

INSPECTION DETAILS

Pollen Gathering		Nectar Flow		Weather	

Purpose for Inspection

DEVELOPMENT TIMES FOR HONEY BEE

Development (days)	Queen	Worker	Drones
Egg hatches after	3	3	3
Cells Capped after	8	8	10
Adults emerge after	16	21	24

HIVE STATUS

Queen Seen		Marked		Eggs	

Queen Cells with Egg, Larva or Pupa		Removed Queen Cells		* Queen Cells Remaining	
Emergency		Spotty Drone Brood		* Frames with Brood	
Swarm		Worker Brood in All Stages		* Frames of Honey/Nectar	
Supersedure		Compact Brood Pattern		* Frames of Pollen	
* Frames bees occupy in brood chamber		* Frames of Foundation		* Frames Open Comb	
		* Supers in place		* Supers added	

HEALTH

Signs of Disease		Good Temper	
Small Hive Beetle Damage			
Nosema Streaking			
Signs of Varroa Mite Infestation			
Feeding and/or Medication			

ACTIONS TAKEN AND NOTES

COLONY CONDITION

Weak		Marginal		Strong	

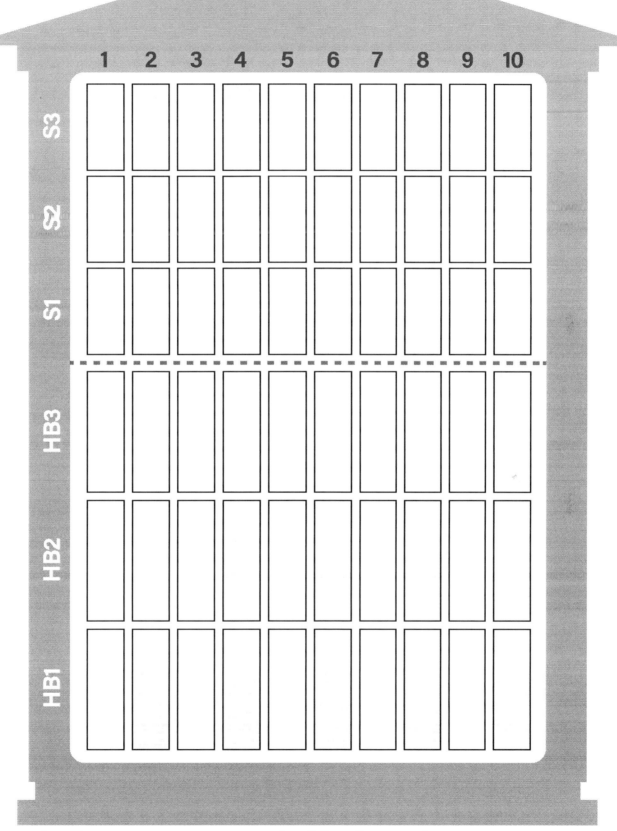

Indicate areas occupied by bees, honey, nectar and pollen. Show the location of vital Queen Cells

HIVE INSPECTION SHEET

Apiary Location:
Hive ID:
Date and Time of Inspection: / / :

INSPECTION DETAILS

Pollen Gathering:
Nectar Flow:
Weather:

Purpose for Inspection

DEVELOPMENT TIMES FOR HONEY BEE

Development (days)	Queen	Worker	Drones
Egg hatches after	3	3	3
Cells Capped after	8	8	10
Adults emerge after	16	21	24

HIVE STATUS

Queen Seen: Marked: Eggs:

Queen Cells with Egg, Larva or Pupa	Removed Queen Cells	* Queen Cells Remaining
Emergency	Spotty Drone Brood	* Frames with Brood
Swarm	Worker Brood in All Stages	* Frames of Honey/Nectar
Supersedure	Compact Brood Pattern	* Frames of Pollen
* Frames bees occupy in brood chamber	* Frames of Foundation	* Frames Open Comb
	* Supers in place	* Supers added

HEALTH

Signs of Disease: Good Temper:
Small Hive Beetle Damage:
Nosema Streaking:
Signs of Varroa Mite Infestation:
Feeding and/or Medication:

ACTIONS TAKEN AND NOTES

COLONY CONDITION

Weak: Marginal: Strong:

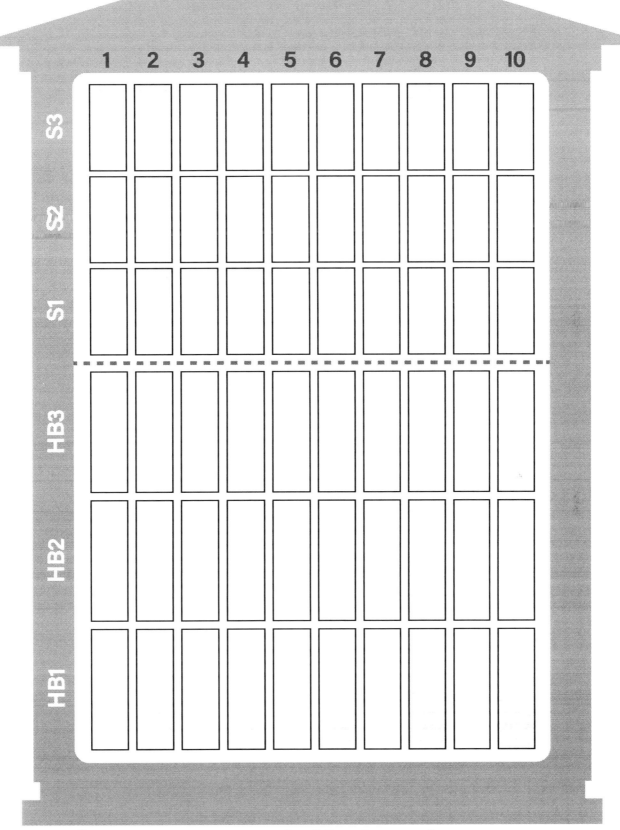

Indicate areas occupied by bees, honey, nectar and pollen. Show the location of vital Queen Cells

HIVE INSPECTION SHEET

Apiary Location: _____   Hive ID: _____

Date and Time of Inspection: __/__/__ :

INSPECTION DETAILS

Pollen Gathering: ____   Nectar Flow: ____   Weather: _____

Purpose for Inspection

DEVELOPMENT TIMES FOR HONEY BEE

Development (days)	Queen	Worker	Drones
Egg hatches after	3	3	3
Cells Capped after	8	8	10
Adults emerge after	16	21	24

HIVE STATUS

Queen Seen: ____   Marked: ____   Eggs: ____

Queen Cells with Egg, Larva or Pupa	Removed Queen Cells	* Queen Cells Remaining
	Spotty Drone Brood	* Frames with Brood
Emergency	Worker Brood in All Stages	* Frames of Honey/Nectar
Swarm	Compact Brood Pattern	* Frames of Pollen
Supersedure	* Frames of Foundation	* Frames Open Comb
* Frames bees occupy in brood chamber	* Supers in place	* Supers added

HEALTH

Signs of Disease: ____   Good Temper: ____

Small Hive Beetle Damage: ____

Nosema Streaking: ____

Signs of Varroa Mite Infestation: ____

Feeding and/or Medication:

ACTIONS TAKEN AND NOTES

COLONY CONDITION

Weak: ____   Marginal: ____   Strong: ____

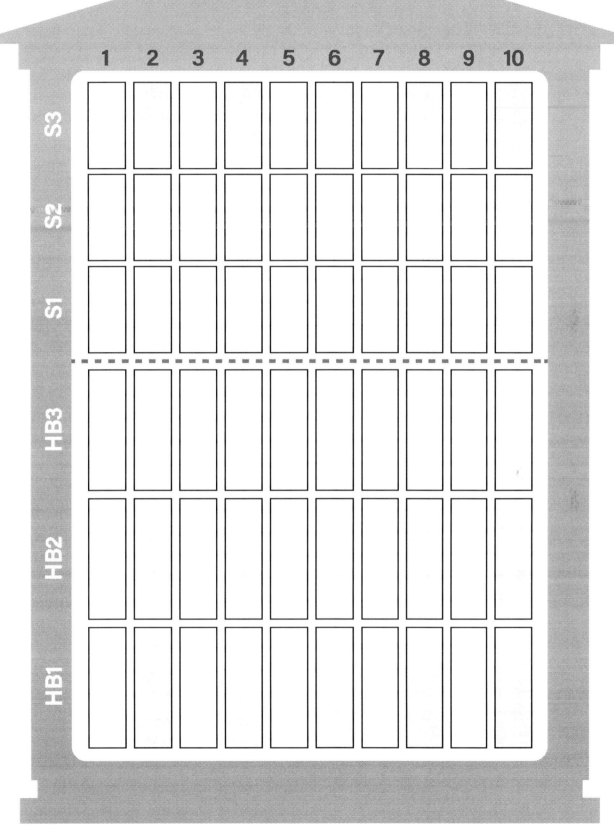

Indicate areas occupied by bees, honey, nectar and pollen. Show the location of vital Queen Cells

HIVE INSPECTION SHEET

Apiary Location:
Hive ID:
Date and Time of Inspection: / / :

INSPECTION DETAILS

Pollen Gathering:
Nectar Flow:
Weather:

Purpose for Inspection

DEVELOPMENT TIMES FOR HONEY BEE

Development (days)	Queen	Worker	Drones
Egg hatches after	3	3	3
Cells Capped after	8	8	10
Adults emerge after	16	21	24

HIVE STATUS

Queen Seen:
Marked:
Eggs:

- Queen Cells with Egg, Larva or Pupa
- Removed Queen Cells
- * Queen Cells Remaining
- Spotty Drone Brood
- * Frames with Brood
- Emergency
- Worker Brood in All Stages
- * Frames of Honey/Nectar
- Swarm
- Compact Brood Pattern
- * Frames of Pollen
- Supersedure
- * Frames of Foundation
- * Frames Open Comb
- * Frames bees occupy in brood chamber
- * Supers in place
- * Supers added

HEALTH

Signs of Disease:
Good Temper:
Small Hive Beetle Damage:
Nosema Streaking:
Signs of Varroa Mite Infestation:
Feeding and/or Medication:

ACTIONS TAKEN AND NOTES

COLONY CONDITION

Weak: Marginal: Strong:

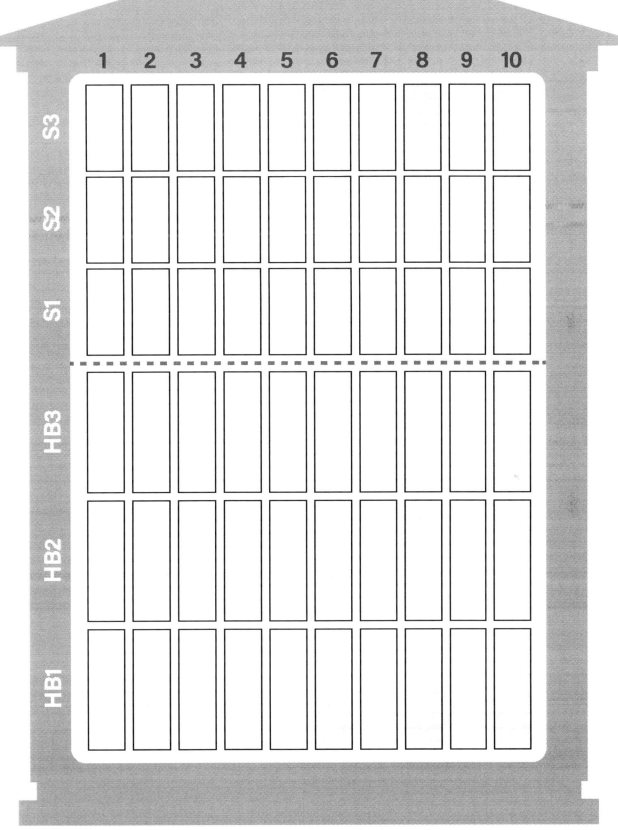

Indicate areas occupied by bees, honey, nectar and pollen. Show the location of vital Queen Cells

HIVE INSPECTION SHEET

Apiary Location: _____
Hive ID: _____
Date and Time of Inspection: ___ / ___ / ___   ___ : ___

INSPECTION DETAILS

Pollen Gathering: ____ **Nectar Flow:** ____ **Weather:** _____

Purpose for Inspection

_____

DEVELOPMENT TIMES FOR HONEY BEE

Development (days)	Queen	Worker	Drones
Egg hatches after	3	3	3
Cells Capped after	8	8	10
Adults emerge after	16	21	24

HIVE STATUS

Queen Seen: ____ **Marked:** ____ **Eggs:** ____

Queen Cells with Egg, Larva or Pupa	Removed Queen Cells	* Queen Cells Remaining
Emergency	Spotty Drone Brood	* Frames with Brood
Swarm	Worker Brood in All Stages	* Frames of Honey/Nectar
Supersedure	Compact Brood Pattern	* Frames of Pollen
* Frames bees occupy in brood chamber	* Frames of Foundation	* Frames Open Comb
	* Supers in place	* Supers added

HEALTH

Signs of Disease: ____ **Good Temper:** ____
Small Hive Beetle Damage: ____
Nosema Streaking: ____
Signs of Varroa Mite Infestation: ____
Feeding and/or Medication:

_____

ACTIONS TAKEN AND NOTES

_____

COLONY CONDITION

Weak: ____ **Marginal:** ____ **Strong:** ____

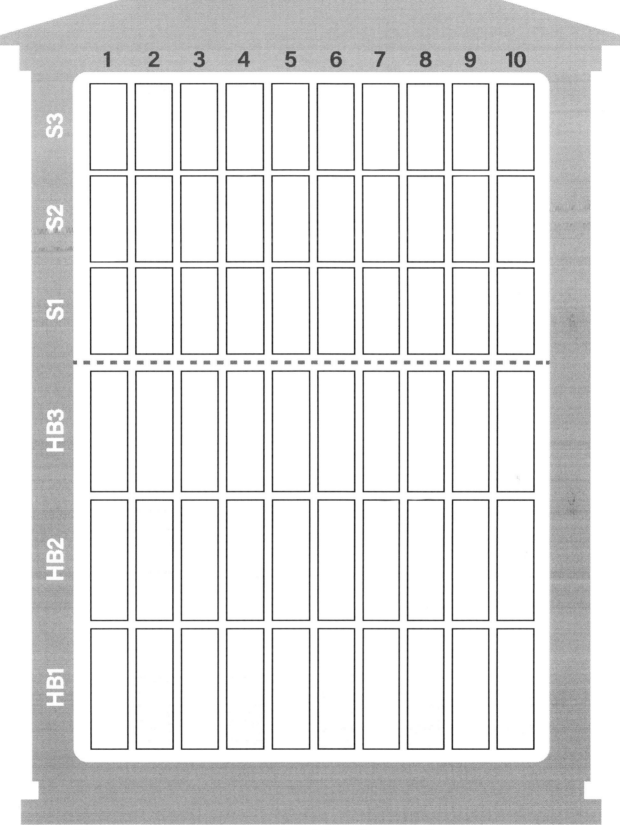

Indicate areas occupied by bees, honey, nectar and pollen. Show the location of vital Queen Cells

HIVE INSPECTION SHEET

Apiary Location: _____ **Hive ID:** _____

Date and Time of Inspection: ___/___/___ : ___

INSPECTION DETAILS

Pollen Gathering: ____ **Nectar Flow:** ____ **Weather:** _____

Purpose for Inspection

_____

DEVELOPMENT TIMES FOR HONEY BEE

Development (days)	Queen	Worker	Drones
Egg hatches after	3	3	3
Cells Capped after	8	8	10
Adults emerge after	16	21	24

HIVE STATUS

Queen Seen: ____ **Marked:** ____ **Eggs:** ____

Queen Cells with Egg, Larva or Pupa	Removed Queen Cells	* Queen Cells Remaining
	Spotty Drone Brood	* Frames with Brood
Emergency	Worker Brood in All Stages	* Frames of Honey/Nectar
Swarm	Compact Brood Pattern	* Frames of Pollen
Supersedure	* Frames of Foundation	* Frames Open Comb
* Frames bees occupy in brood chamber	* Supers in place	* Supers added

HEALTH

Signs of Disease: ____ **Good Temper:** ____

Small Hive Beetle Damage: ____

Nosema Streaking: ____

Signs of Varroa Mite Infestation: ____

Feeding and/or Medication:

_____

ACTIONS TAKEN AND NOTES

_____

COLONY CONDITION

Weak: ____ **Marginal:** ____ **Strong:** ____

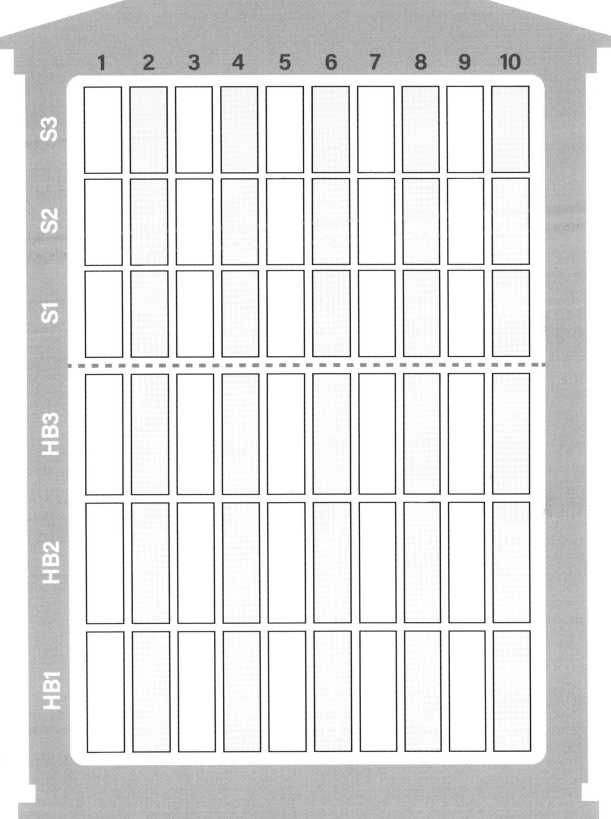

Indicate areas occupied by bees, honey, nectar and pollen. Show the location of vital Queen Cells

HIVE INSPECTION SHEET

Apiary Location: _____   Hive ID: _____

Date and Time of Inspection: ___/___/___   : ____

INSPECTION DETAILS

Pollen Gathering: ____   Nectar Flow: ____   Weather: _____

Purpose for Inspection

_____

DEVELOPMENT TIMES FOR HONEY BEE

Development (days)	Queen	Worker	Drones
Egg hatches after	3	3	3
Cells Capped after	8	8	10
Adults emerge after	16	21	24

HIVE STATUS

Queen Seen: ____   Marked: ____   Eggs: ____

Queen Cells with Egg, Larva or Pupa	Removed Queen Cells	* Queen Cells Remaining
Emergency	Spotty Drone Brood	* Frames with Brood
Swarm	Worker Brood in All Stages	* Frames of Honey/Nectar
Supersedure	Compact Brood Pattern	* Frames of Pollen
* Frames bees occupy in brood chamber	* Frames of Foundation	* Frames Open Comb
	* Supers in place	* Supers added

HEALTH

Signs of Disease: ____   Good Temper: ____

Small Hive Beetle Damage: ____

Nosema Streaking: ____

Signs of Varroa Mite Infestation: ____

Feeding and/or Medication:

_____

ACTIONS TAKEN AND NOTES

_____

COLONY CONDITION

Weak: ____   Marginal: ____   Strong: ____

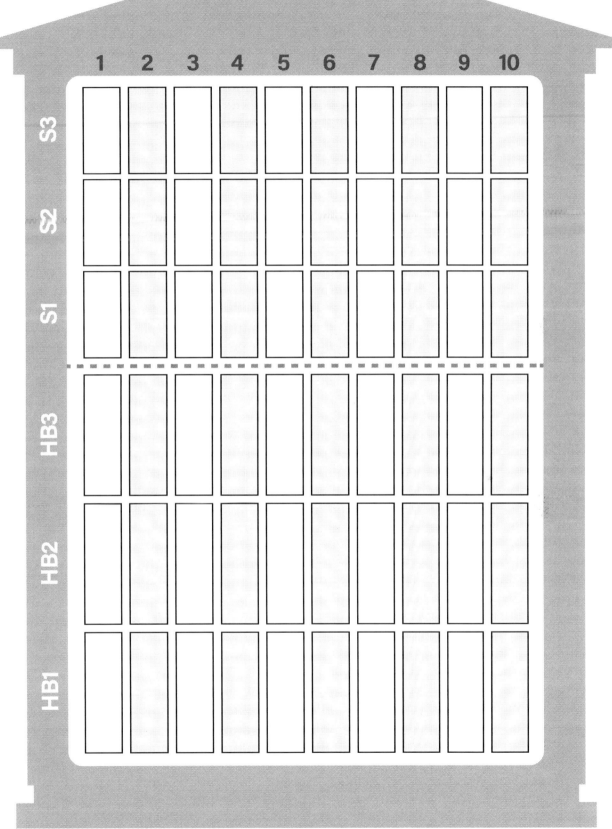

Indicate areas occupied by bees, honey, nectar and pollen. Show the location of vital Queen Cells

HIVE INSPECTION SHEET

Apiary Location: _____
Hive ID: _____
Date and Time of Inspection: __/__/__ __:__

INSPECTION DETAILS

Pollen Gathering: ___ **Nectar Flow:** ___ **Weather:** _____

Purpose for Inspection

_____

DEVELOPMENT TIMES FOR HONEY BEE

Development (days)	Queen	Worker	Drones
Egg hatches after	3	3	3
Cells Capped after	8	8	10
Adults emerge after	16	21	24

HIVE STATUS

Queen Seen: ___ **Marked:** ___ **Eggs:** ___

Queen Cells with Egg, Larva or Pupa	Removed Queen Cells	* Queen Cells Remaining
	Spotty Drone Brood	* Frames with Brood
Emergency	Worker Brood in All Stages	* Frames of Honey/Nectar
Swarm	Compact Brood Pattern	* Frames of Pollen
Supersedure	* Frames of Foundation	* Frames Open Comb
* Frames bees occupy in brood chamber	* Supers in place	* Supers added

HEALTH

Signs of Disease: ___ **Good Temper:** ___
Small Hive Beetle Damage: ___
Nosema Streaking: ___
Signs of Varroa Mite Infestation: ___

Feeding and/or Medication

_____

ACTIONS TAKEN AND NOTES

_____

COLONY CONDITION

Weak: ___ **Marginal:** ___ **Strong:** ___

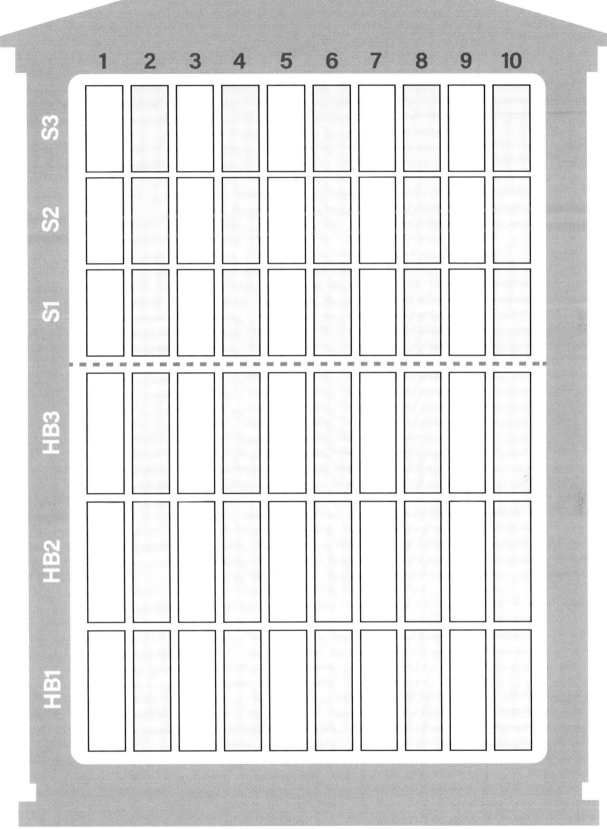

Indicate areas occupied by bees, honey, nectar and pollen. Show the location of vital Queen Cells

HIVE INSPECTION SHEET

Apiary Location:
Hive ID:
Date and Time of Inspection: / / :

INSPECTION DETAILS

Pollen Gathering:
Nectar Flow:
Weather:

Purpose for Inspection

DEVELOPMENT TIMES FOR HONEY BEE

Development (days)	Queen	Worker	Drones
Egg hatches after	3	3	3
Cells Capped after	8	8	10
Adults emerge after	16	21	24

HIVE STATUS

Queen Seen:
Marked:
Eggs:

Queen Cells with Egg, Larva or Pupa	Removed Queen Cells	* Queen Cells Remaining
	Spotty Drone Brood	* Frames with Brood
Emergency	Worker Brood in All Stages	* Frames of Honey/Nectar
Swarm	Compact Brood Pattern	* Frames of Pollen
Supersedure	* Frames of Foundation	* Frames Open Comb
* Frames bees occupy in brood chamber	* Supers in place	* Supers added

HEALTH

Signs of Disease:
Good Temper:
Small Hive Beetle Damage:
Nosema Streaking:
Signs of Varroa Mite Infestation:

Feeding and/or Medication

ACTIONS TAKEN AND NOTES

COLONY CONDITION

Weak | Marginal | Strong

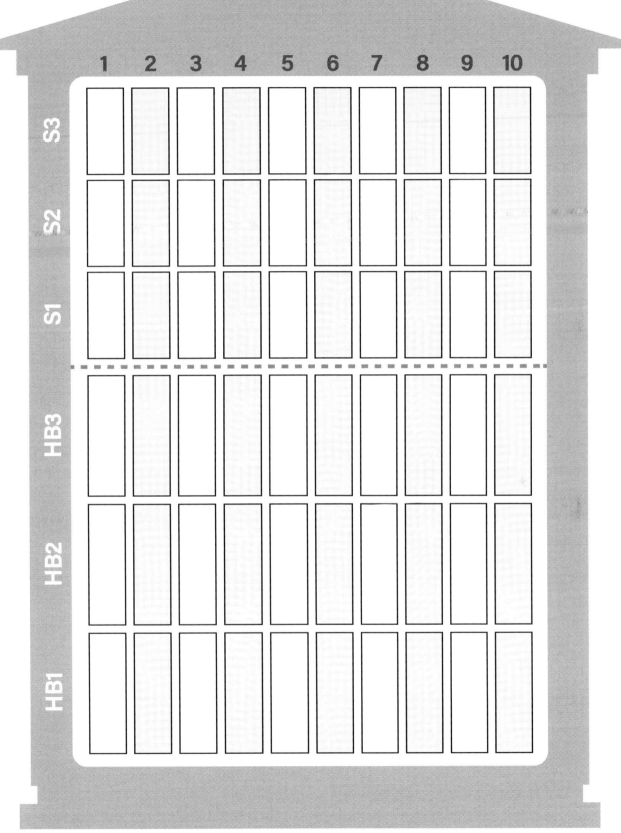

Indicate areas occupied by bees, honey, nectar and pollen. Show the location of vital Queen Cells

HIVE INSPECTION SHEET

Apiary Location: _____
Hive ID: _____
Date and Time of Inspection: ___/___/___   ___:___

INSPECTION DETAILS

Pollen Gathering: ____   **Nectar Flow:** ____   **Weather:** _____

Purpose for Inspection

_____

DEVELOPMENT TIMES FOR HONEY BEE

Development (days)	Queen	Worker	Drones
Egg hatches after	3	3	3
Cells Capped after	8	8	10
Adults emerge after	16	21	24

HIVE STATUS

Queen Seen ____   Marked ____   Eggs ____

Queen Cells with Egg, Larva or Pupa	Removed Queen Cells	* Queen Cells Remaining
	Spotty Drone Brood	* Frames with Brood
Emergency	Worker Brood in All Stages	* Frames of Honey/Nectar
Swarm	Compact Brood Pattern	* Frames of Pollen
Supersedure	* Frames of Foundation	* Frames Open Comb
* Frames bees occupy in brood chamber	* Supers in place	* Supers added

HEALTH

Signs of Disease ____   Good Temper ____
Small Hive Beetle Damage ____
Nosema Streaking ____
Signs of Varroa Mite Infestation ____
Feeding and/or Medication
_____

ACTIONS TAKEN AND NOTES

_____

COLONY CONDITION

Weak ____   Marginal ____   Strong ____

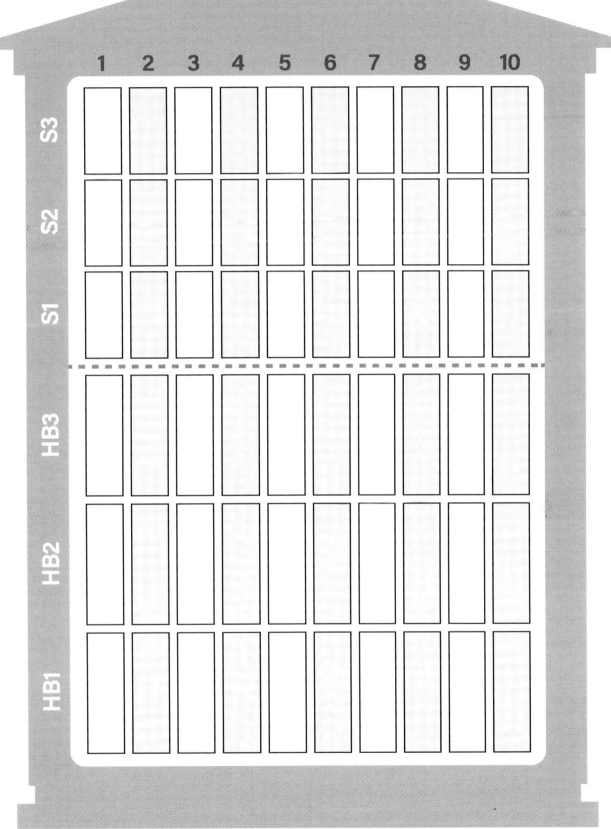

Indicate areas occupied by bees, honey, nectar and pollen. Show the location of vital Queen Cells

HIVE INSPECTION SHEET

Apiary Location: _____
Hive ID: _____
Date and Time of Inspection: __/__/__ __:__

INSPECTION DETAILS

Pollen Gathering: ____   Nectar Flow: ____   Weather: _____

Purpose for Inspection

_____

DEVELOPMENT TIMES FOR HONEY BEE

Development (days)	Queen	Worker	Drones
Egg hatches after	3	3	3
Cells Capped after	8	8	10
Adults emerge after	16	21	24

HIVE STATUS

Queen Seen: ____   Marked: ____   Eggs: ____

Queen Cells with Egg, Larva or Pupa	Removed Queen Cells	* Queen Cells Remaining
Emergency	Spotty Drone Brood	* Frames with Brood
Swarm	Worker Brood in All Stages	* Frames of Honey/Nectar
Supersedure	Compact Brood Pattern	* Frames of Pollen
* Frames bees occupy in brood chamber	* Frames of Foundation	* Frames Open Comb
	* Supers in place	* Supers added

HEALTH

Signs of Disease: ____   Good Temper: ____
Small Hive Beetle Damage: ____
Nosema Streaking: ____
Signs of Varroa Mite Infestation: ____
Feeding and/or Medication: ____

_____

ACTIONS TAKEN AND NOTES

_____

COLONY CONDITION

Weak: ____   Marginal: ____   Strong: ____

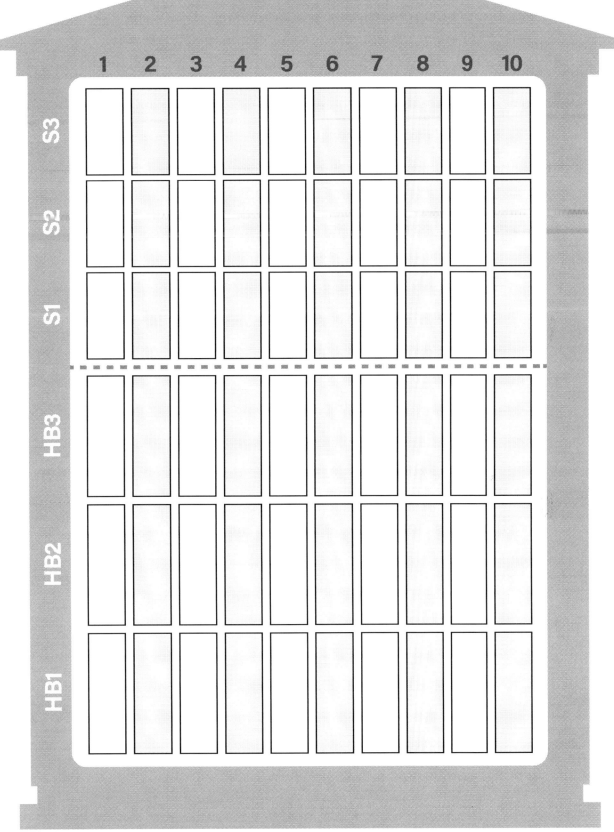

Indicate areas occupied by bees, honey, nectar and pollen. Show the location of vital Queen Cells

HIVE INSPECTION SHEET

Apiary Location: _____ Hive ID: _____

Date and Time of Inspection: __/__/__ : __

INSPECTION DETAILS

Pollen Gathering: ____ Nectar Flow: ____ Weather: _____

Purpose for Inspection:

DEVELOPMENT TIMES FOR HONEY BEE

Development (days)	Queen	Worker	Drones
Egg hatches after	3	3	3
Cells Capped after	8	8	10
Adults emerge after	16	21	24

HIVE STATUS

Queen Seen: ____ Marked: ____ Eggs: ____

Queen Cells with Egg, Larva or Pupa	Removed Queen Cells	* Queen Cells Remaining
	Spotty Drone Brood	* Frames with Brood
Emergency	Worker Brood in All Stages	* Frames of Honey/Nectar
Swarm	Compact Brood Pattern	* Frames of Pollen
Supersedure	* Frames of Foundation	* Frames Open Comb
* Frames bees occupy in brood chamber	* Supers in place	* Supers added

HEALTH

Signs of Disease: ____ Good Temper: ____

Small Hive Beetle Damage: ____

Nosema Streaking: ____

Signs of Varroa Mite Infestation: ____

Feeding and/or Medication:

ACTIONS TAKEN AND NOTES

COLONY CONDITION

Weak: ____ Marginal: ____ Strong: ____

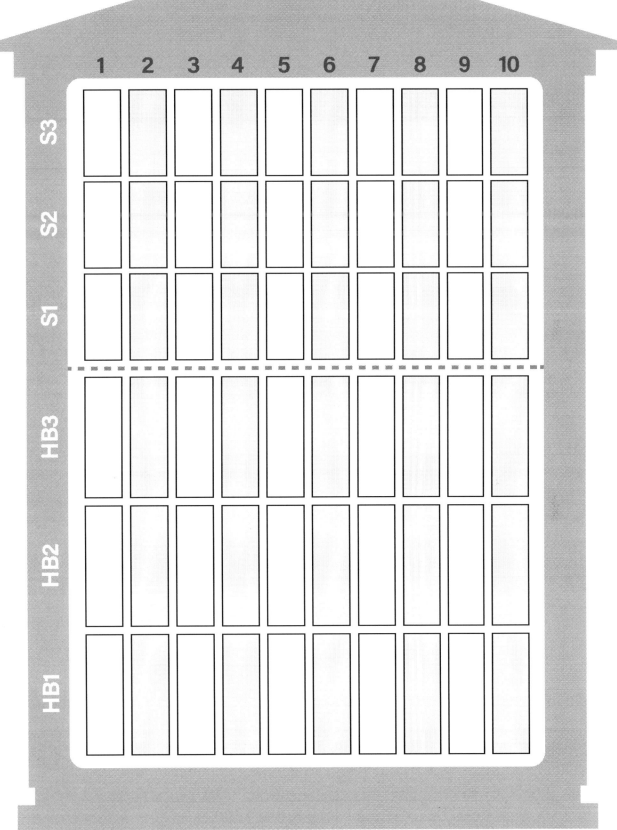

Indicate areas occupied by bees, honey, nectar and pollen. Show the location of vital Queen Cells

HIVE INSPECTION SHEET

Apiary Location:
Hive ID:
Date and Time of Inspection: / / :

INSPECTION DETAILS

Pollen Gathering:
Nectar Flow:
Weather:

Purpose for Inspection

DEVELOPMENT TIMES FOR HONEY BEE

Development (days)	Queen	Worker	Drones
Egg hatches after	3	3	3
Cells Capped after	8	8	10
Adults emerge after	16	21	24

HIVE STATUS

Queen Seen: **Marked:** **Eggs:**

- Queen Cells with Egg, Larva or Pupa
- Removed Queen Cells
- * Queen Cells Remaining
- Spotty Drone Brood
- * Frames with Brood
- Emergency
- Worker Brood in All Stages
- * Frames of Honey/Nectar
- Swarm
- Compact Brood Pattern
- * Frames of Pollen
- Supersedure
- * Frames of Foundation
- * Frames Open Comb
- * Frames bees occupy in brood chamber
- * Supers in place
- * Supers added

HEALTH

- Signs of Disease
- Good Temper
- Small Hive Beetle Damage
- Nosema Streaking
- Signs of Varroa Mite Infestation
- Feeding and/or Medication

ACTIONS TAKEN AND NOTES

COLONY CONDITION

Weak **Marginal** **Strong**

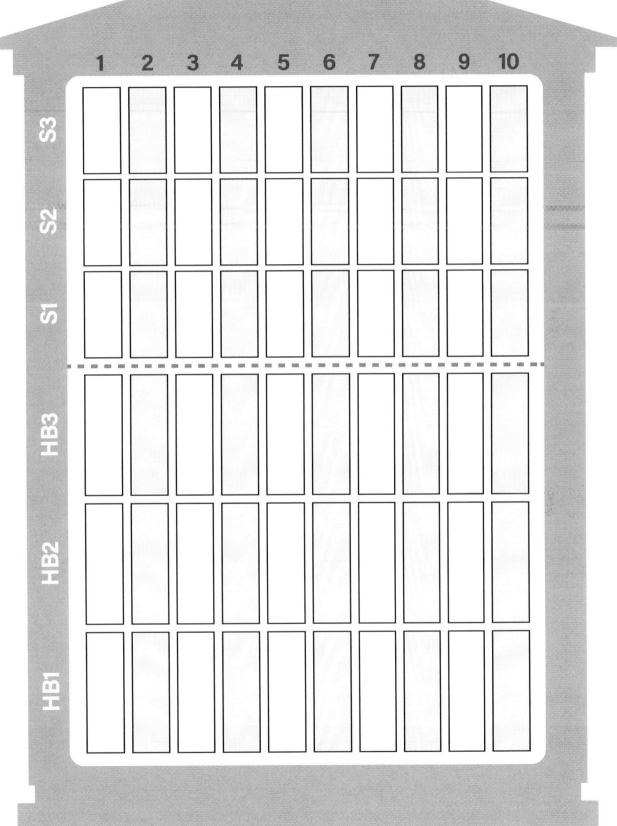

Indicate areas occupied by bees, honey, nectar and pollen. Show the location of vital Queen Cells

HIVE INSPECTION SHEET

Apiary Location: _____

Hive ID: _____

Date and Time of Inspection: __/__/__ : __

INSPECTION DETAILS

Pollen Gathering: ___ Nectar Flow: ___ Weather: _____

Purpose for Inspection

_____

DEVELOPMENT TIMES FOR HONEY BEE

Development (days)	Queen	Worker	Drones
Egg hatches after	3	3	3
Cells Capped after	8	8	10
Adults emerge after	16	21	24

HIVE STATUS

Queen Seen: ___   Marked: ___   Eggs: ___

Queen Cells with Egg, Larva or Pupa	Removed Queen Cells	* Queen Cells Remaining
	Spotty Drone Brood	* Frames with Brood
Emergency	Worker Brood in All Stages	* Frames of Honey/Nectar
Swarm	Compact Brood Pattern	* Frames of Pollen
Supersedure	* Frames of Foundation	* Frames Open Comb
* Frames bees occupy in brood chamber	* Supers in place	* Supers added

HEALTH

Signs of Disease: ___   Good Temper: ___

Small Hive Beetle Damage: ___

Nosema Streaking: ___

Signs of Varroa Mite Infestation: ___

Feeding and/or Medication:

_____

ACTIONS TAKEN AND NOTES

_____

COLONY CONDITION

Weak: ___   Marginal: ___   Strong: ___

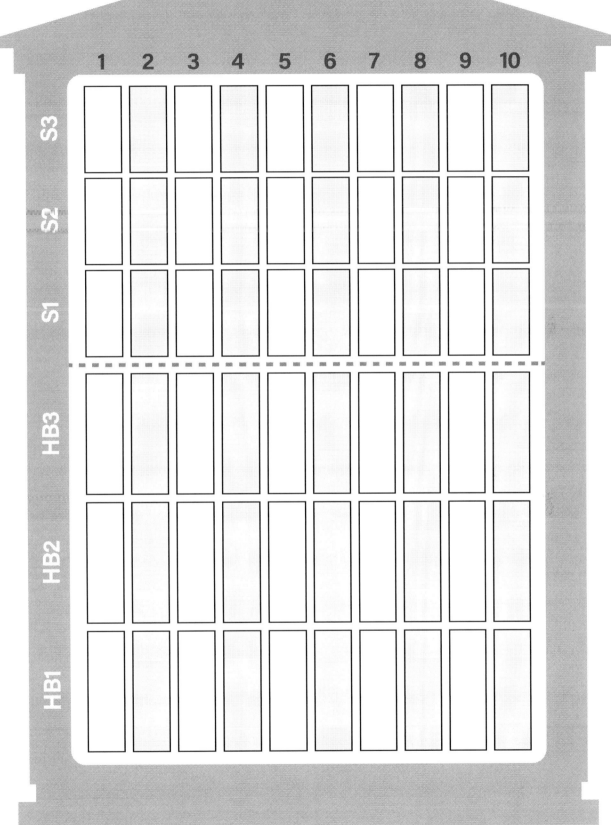

Indicate areas occupied by bees, honey, nectar and pollen. Show the location of vital Queen Cells

HIVE INSPECTION SHEET

Apiary Location: _____
Date and Time of Inspection: __/__/__ __:__
Hive ID: _____

INSPECTION DETAILS

Pollen Gathering: ___ **Nectar Flow:** ___ **Weather:** _____

Purpose for Inspection

_____

DEVELOPMENT TIMES FOR HONEY BEE

Development (days)	Queen	Worker	Drones
Egg hatches after	3	3	3
Cells Capped after	8	8	10
Adults emerge after	16	21	24

HIVE STATUS

Queen Seen: ___ **Marked:** ___ **Eggs:** ___

Queen Cells with Egg, Larva or Pupa	Removed Queen Cells	* Queen Cells Remaining
Emergency	Spotty Drone Brood	* Frames with Brood
Swarm	Worker Brood in All Stages	* Frames of Honey/Nectar
Supersedure	Compact Brood Pattern	* Frames of Pollen
* Frames bees occupy in brood chamber	* Frames of Foundation	* Frames Open Comb
	* Supers in place	* Supers added

HEALTH

Signs of Disease: ___ **Good Temper:** ___
Small Hive Beetle Damage: ___
Nosema Streaking: ___
Signs of Varroa Mite Infestation: ___

Feeding and/or Medication

_____

ACTIONS TAKEN AND NOTES

_____

COLONY CONDITION

Weak: ___ **Marginal:** ___ **Strong:** ___

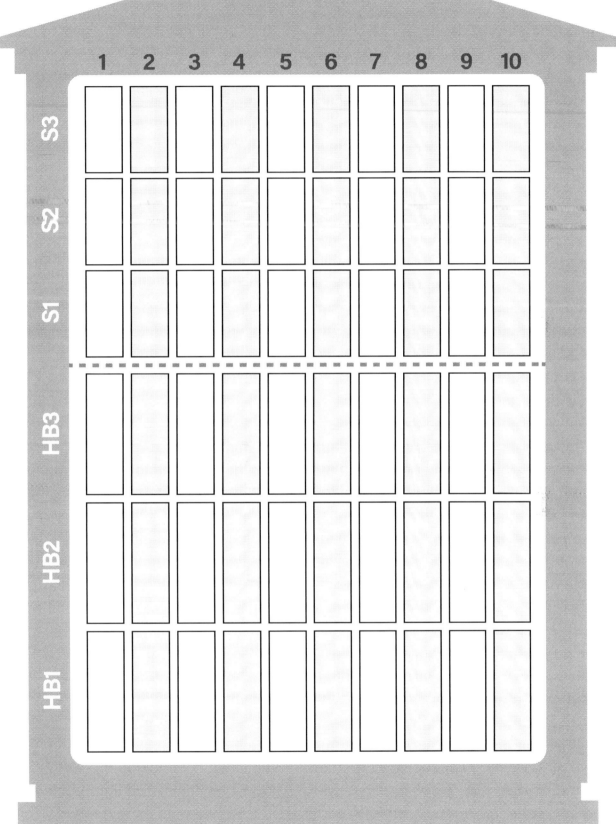

Indicate areas occupied by bees, honey, nectar and pollen. Show the location of vital Queen Cells

HIVE INSPECTION SHEET

Apiary Location:
Hive ID:
Date and Time of Inspection: /   /   :

INSPECTION DETAILS

Pollen Gathering:
Nectar Flow:
Weather:

Purpose for Inspection

DEVELOPMENT TIMES FOR HONEY BEE

Development (days)	Queen	Worker	Drones
Egg hatches after	3	3	3
Cells Capped after	8	8	10
Adults emerge after	16	21	24

HIVE STATUS

Queen Seen: Marked: Eggs:

Queen Cells with Egg, Larva or Pupa	Removed Queen Cells	* Queen Cells Remaining
	Spotty Drone Brood	* Frames with Brood
Emergency	Worker Brood in All Stages	* Frames of Honey/Nectar
Swarm	Compact Brood Pattern	* Frames of Pollen
Supersedure	* Frames of Foundation	* Frames Open Comb
* Frames bees occupy in brood chamber	* Supers in place	* Supers added

HEALTH

Signs of Disease: Good Temper:
Small Hive Beetle Damage:
Nosema Streaking:
Signs of Varroa Mite Infestation:
Feeding and/or Medication:

ACTIONS TAKEN AND NOTES

COLONY CONDITION

Weak: Marginal: Strong:

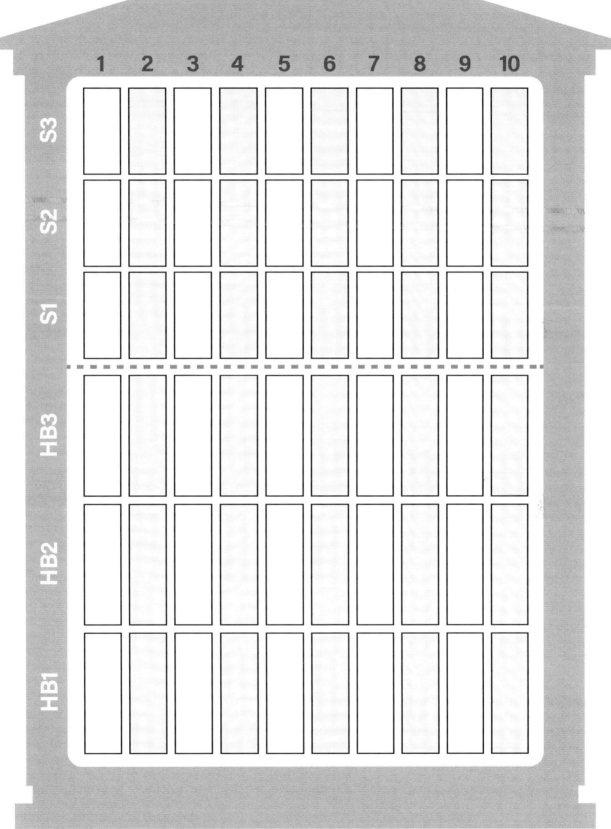

Indicate areas occupied by bees, honey, nectar and pollen. Show the location of vital Queen Cells

HIVE INSPECTION SHEET

Apiary Location:
Date and Time of Inspection: / / :
Hive ID:

INSPECTION DETAILS

Pollen Gathering:
Nectar Flow:
Weather:

Purpose for Inspection

DEVELOPMENT TIMES FOR HONEY BEE

Development (days)	Queen	Worker	Drones
Egg hatches after	3	3	3
Cells Capped after	8	8	10
Adults emerge after	16	21	24

HIVE STATUS

Queen Seen:
Marked:
Eggs:

Queen Cells with Egg, Larva or Pupa	Removed Queen Cells	* Queen Cells Remaining
Emergency	Spotty Drone Brood	* Frames with Brood
Swarm	Worker Brood in All Stages	* Frames of Honey/Nectar
Supersedure	Compact Brood Pattern	* Frames of Pollen
* Frames bees occupy in brood chamber	* Frames of Foundation	* Frames Open Comb
	* Supers in place	* Supers added

HEALTH

Signs of Disease:
Good Temper:
Small Hive Beetle Damage:
Nosema Streaking:
Signs of Varroa Mite Infestation:
Feeding and/or Medication:

ACTIONS TAKEN AND NOTES

COLONY CONDITION

Weak:
Marginal:
Strong:

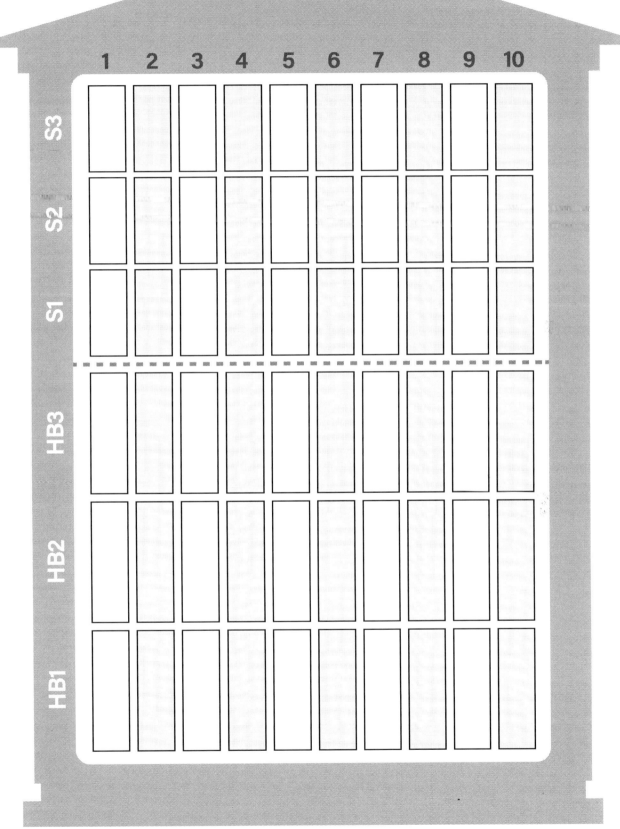

Indicate areas occupied by bees, honey, nectar and pollen. Show the location of vital Queen Cells

2021

JANUARY
SUN	MON	TUE	WED	THU	FRI	SAT
					1	2
3	4	5	6	7	8	9
10	11	12	13	14	15	16
17	18	19	20	21	22	23
24	25	26	27	28	29	30
31						

FEBRUARY
SUN	MON	TUE	WED	THU	FRI	SAT
	1	2	3	4	5	6
7	8	9	10	11	12	13
14	15	16	17	18	19	20
21	22	23	24	25	26	27
28						

MARCH
SUN	MON	TUE	WED	THU	FRI	SAT
	1	2	3	4	5	6
7	8	9	10	11	12	13
14	15	16	17	18	19	20
21	22	23	24	25	26	27
28	29	30	31			

APRIL
SUN	MON	TUE	WED	THU	FRI	SAT
				1	2	3
4	5	6	7	8	9	10
11	12	13	14	15	16	17
18	19	20	21	22	23	24
25	26	27	28	29	30	

MAY
SUN	MON	TUE	WED	THU	FRI	SAT
						1
2	3	4	5	6	7	8
9	10	11	12	13	14	15
16	17	18	19	20	21	22
23	24	25	26	27	28	29
30	31					

JUNE
SUN	MON	TUE	WED	THU	FRI	SAT
		1	2	3	4	5
6	7	8	9	10	11	12
13	14	15	16	17	18	19
20	21	22	23	24	25	26
27	28	29	30			

JULY
SUN	MON	TUE	WED	THU	FRI	SAT
				1	2	3
4	5	6	7	8	9	10
11	12	13	14	15	16	17
18	19	20	21	22	23	24
25	26	27	28	29	30	31

AUGUST
SUN	MON	TUE	WED	THU	FRI	SAT
1	2	3	4	5	6	7
8	9	10	11	12	13	14
15	16	17	18	19	20	21
22	23	24	25	26	27	28
29	30	31				

SEPTEMBER
SUN	MON	TUE	WED	THU	FRI	SAT
			1	2	3	4
5	6	7	8	9	10	11
12	13	14	15	16	17	18
19	20	21	22	23	24	25
26	27	28	29	30		

OCTOBER
SUN	MON	TUE	WED	THU	FRI	SAT
					1	2
3	4	5	6	7	8	9
10	11	12	13	14	15	16
17	18	19	20	21	22	23
24	25	26	27	28	29	30
31						

NOVEMBER
SUN	MON	TUE	WED	THU	FRI	SAT
	1	2	3	4	5	6
7	8	9	10	11	12	13
14	15	16	17	18	19	20
21	22	23	24	25	26	27
28	29	30				

DECEMBER
SUN	MON	TUE	WED	THU	FRI	SAT
			1	2	3	4
5	6	7	8	9	10	11
12	13	14	15	16	17	18
19	20	21	22	23	24	25
26	27	28	29	30	31	

*JAN 2021

SUNDAY	MONDAY	TUESDAY
3	4	5
10	11	12
17	18	19
24	25	26
31		

NOTE

○
○
○
○
○
○
○
○
○
○

JANUARY 2021
SUN	MON	TUE	WED	THU	FRI	SAT
					1	2
3	4	5	6	7	8	9
10	11	12	13	14	15	16
17	18	19	20	21	22	23
24	25	26	27	28	29	30
31						

FEBRUARY 2021
SUN	MON	TUE	WED	THU	FRI	SAT
	1	2	3	4	5	6
7	8	9	10	11	12	13
14	15	16	17	18	19	20
21	22	23	24	25	26	27
28						

MARCH 2021
SUN	MON	TUE	WED	THU	FRI	SAT
	1	2	3	4	5	6
7	8	9	10	11	12	13
14	15	16	17	18	19	20
21	22	23	24	25	26	27
28	29	30	31			

APRIL 2021
SUN	MON	TUE	WED	THU	FRI	SAT
				1	2	3
4	5	6	7	8	9	10
11	12	13	14	15	16	17
18	19	20	21	22	23	24
25	26	27	28	29	30	

MAY 2021
SUN	MON	TUE	WED	THU	FRI	SAT
						1
2	3	4	5	6	7	8
9	10	11	12	13	14	15
16	17	18	19	20	21	22
23	24	25	26	27	28	29
30	31					

JUNE 2021
SUN	MON	TUE	WED	THU	FRI	SAT
		1	2	3	4	5
6	7	8	9	10	11	12
13	14	15	16	17	18	19
20	21	22	23	24	25	26
27	28	29	30			

WEDNESDAY	THURSDAY	FRIDAY	SATURDAY
		1	2
6	7	8	9
13	14	15	16
20	21	22	23
27	28	29	30

JULY 2021

SUN	MON	TUE	WED	THU	FRI	SAT
				1	2	3
4	5	6	7	8	9	10
11	12	13	14	15	16	17
18	19	20	21	22	23	24
25	26	27	28	29	30	31

AUGUST 2021

SUN	MON	TUE	WED	THU	FRI	SAT
1	2	3	4	5	6	7
8	9	10	11	12	13	14
15	16	17	18	19	20	21
22	23	24	25	26	27	28
29	30	31				

SEPTEMBER 2021

SUN	MON	TUE	WED	THU	FRI	SAT
			1	2	3	4
5	6	7	8	9	10	11
12	13	14	15	16	17	18
19	20	21	22	23	24	25
26	27	28	29	30		

OCTOBER 2021

SUN	MON	TUE	WED	THU	FRI	SAT
					1	2
3	4	5	6	7	8	9
10	11	12	13	14	15	16
17	18	19	20	21	22	23
24	25	26	27	28	29	30
31						

NOVEMBER 2021

SUN	MON	TUE	WED	THU	FRI	SAT
	1	2	3	4	5	6
7	8	9	10	11	12	13
14	15	16	17	18	19	20
21	22	23	24	25	26	27
28	29	30				

DECEMBER 2021

SUN	MON	TUE	WED	THU	FRI	SAT
			1	2	3	4
5	6	7	8	9	10	11
12	13	14	15	16	17	18
19	20	21	22	23	24	25
26	27	28	29	30	31	

*FEB 2021

NOTE

SUNDAY	MONDAY	TUESDAY
	1	2
7	8	9
14	15	16
21	22	23
28		

JANUARY 2021	FEBRUARY 2021	MARCH 2021	APRIL 2021	MAY 2021	JUNE 2021
SUN MON TUE WED THU FRI SAT	SUN MON TUE WED THU FRI SAT	SUN MON TUE WED THU FRI SAT	SUN MON TUE WED THU FRI SAT	SUN MON TUE WED THU FRI SAT	SUN MON TUE WED THU FRI SAT
1 2	1 2 3 4 5 6	1 2 3 4 5 6	1 2 3	1	1 2 3 4 5
3 4 5 6 7 8 9	7 8 9 10 11 12 13	7 8 9 10 11 12 13	4 5 6 7 8 9 10	2 3 4 5 6 7 8	6 7 8 9 10 11 12
10 11 12 13 14 15 16	14 15 16 17 18 19 20	14 15 16 17 18 19 20	11 12 13 14 15 16 17	9 10 11 12 13 14 15	13 14 15 16 17 18 19
17 18 19 20 21 22 23	21 22 23 24 25 26 27	21 22 23 24 25 26 27	18 19 20 21 22 23 24	16 17 18 19 20 21 22	20 21 22 23 24 25 26
24 25 26 27 28 29 30	28	28 29 30 31	25 26 27 28 29 30	23 24 25 26 27 28 29	27 28 29 30
31				30 31	

WEDNESDAY	THURSDAY	FRIDAY	SATURDAY
3	4	5	6
10	11	12	13
17	18	19	20
24	25	26	27

JULY 2021
SUN	MON	TUE	WED	THU	FRI	SAT
				1	2	3
4	5	6	7	8	9	10
11	12	13	14	15	16	17
18	19	20	21	22	23	24
25	26	27	28	29	30	31

AUGUST 2021
SUN	MON	TUE	WED	THU	FRI	SAT
1	2	3	4	5	6	7
8	9	10	11	12	13	14
15	16	17	18	19	20	21
22	23	24	25	26	27	28
29	30	31				

SEPTEMBER 2021
SUN	MON	TUE	WED	THU	FRI	SAT
			1	2	3	4
5	6	7	8	9	10	11
12	13	14	15	16	17	18
19	20	21	22	23	24	25
26	27	28	29	30		

OCTOBER 2021
SUN	MON	TUE	WED	THU	FRI	SAT
					1	2
3	4	5	6	7	8	9
10	11	12	13	14	15	16
17	18	19	20	21	22	23
24	25	26	27	28	29	30
31						

NOVEMBER 2021
SUN	MON	TUE	WED	THU	FRI	SAT
	1	2	3	4	5	6
7	8	9	10	11	12	13
14	15	16	17	18	19	20
21	22	23	24	25	26	27
28	29	30				

DECEMBER 2021
SUN	MON	TUE	WED	THU	FRI	SAT
			1	2	3	4
5	6	7	8	9	10	11
12	13	14	15	16	17	18
19	20	21	22	23	24	25
26	27	28	29	30	31	

*MAR 2021

SUNDAY	MONDAY	TUESDAY
	1	2
7	8	9
14	15	16
21	22	23
28	29	30

NOTE

JANUARY 2021	FEBRUARY 2021	MARCH 2021	APRIL 2021	MAY 2021	JUNE 2021
SUN MON TUE WED THU FRI SAT	SUN MON TUE WED THU FRI SAT	SUN MON TUE WED THU FRI SAT	SUN MON TUE WED THU FRI SAT	SUN MON TUE WED THU FRI SAT	SUN MON TUE WED THU FRI SAT
1 2	1 2 3 4 5 6	1 2 3 4 5 6	1 2 3	1	1 2 3 4
3 4 5 6 7 8 9	7 8 9 10 11 12 13	7 8 9 10 11 12 13	4 5 6 7 8 9 10	2 3 4 5 6 7 8	6 7 8 9 10 11 12
10 11 12 13 14 15 16	14 15 16 17 18 19 20	14 15 16 17 18 19 20	11 12 13 14 15 16 17	9 10 11 12 13 14 15	13 14 15 16 17 18 19
17 18 19 20 21 22 23	21 22 23 24 25 26 27	21 22 23 24 25 26 27	18 19 20 21 22 23 24	16 17 18 19 20 21 22	20 21 22 23 24 25 26
24 25 26 27 28 29 30	28	28 29 30 31	25 26 27 28 29 30	23 24 25 26 27 28 29	27 28 29 30
31				30 31	

WEDNESDAY	THURSDAY	FRIDAY	SATURDAY
3	4	5	6
10	11	12	13
17	18	19	20
24	25	26	27
31			

*APR 2021

SUNDAY	MONDAY	TUESDAY
4	5	6
11	12	13
18	19	20
25	26	27

NOTE

- ○
- ○
- ○
- ○
- ○
- ○
- ○
- ○
- ○
- ○

JANUARY 2021	FEBRUARY 2021	MARCH 2021	APRIL 2021	MAY 2021	JUNE 2021
Sun Mon Tue Wed Thu Fri Sat	Sun Mon Tue Wed Thu Fri Sat	Sun Mon Tue Wed Thu Fri Sat	Sun Mon Tue Wed Thu Fri Sat	Sun Mon Tue Wed Thu Fri Sat	Sun Mon Tue Wed Thu Fri Sat
1 2	1 2 3 4 5 6	1 2 3 4 5 6	1 2 3	1	1 2 3 4 5
3 4 5 6 7 8 9	7 8 9 10 11 12 13	7 8 9 10 11 12 13	4 5 6 7 8 9 10	2 3 4 5 6 7 8	6 7 8 9 10 11 12
10 11 12 13 14 15 16	14 15 16 17 18 19 20	14 15 16 17 18 19 20	11 12 13 14 15 16 17	9 10 11 12 13 14 15	13 14 15 16 17 18 19
17 18 19 20 21 22 23	21 22 23 24 25 26 27	21 22 23 24 25 26 27	18 19 20 21 22 23 24	16 17 18 19 20 21 22	20 21 22 23 24 25 26
24 25 26 27 28 29 30	28	28 29 30 31	25 26 27 28 29 30	23 24 25 26 27 28 29	27 28 29 30
31				30 31	

WEDNESDAY	THURSDAY	FRIDAY	SATURDAY
	1	2	3
7	8	9	10
14	15	16	17
21	22	23	24
28	29	30	

JULY 2021
SUN	MON	TUE	WED	THU	FRI	SAT
				1	2	3
4	5	6	7	8	9	10
11	12	13	14	15	16	17
18	19	20	21	22	23	24
25	26	27	28	29	30	31

AUGUST 2021
SUN	MON	TUE	WED	THU	FRI	SAT
1	2	3	4	5	6	7
8	9	10	11	12	13	14
15	16	17	18	19	20	21
22	23	24	25	26	27	28
29	30	31				

SEPTEMBER 2021
SUN	MON	TUE	WED	THU	FRI	SAT
			1	2	3	4
5	6	7	8	9	10	11
12	13	14	15	16	17	18
19	20	21	22	23	24	25
26	27	28	29	30		

OCTOBER 2021
SUN	MON	TUE	WED	THU	FRI	SAT
					1	2
3	4	5	6	7	8	9
10	11	12	13	14	15	16
17	18	19	20	21	22	23
24	25	26	27	28	29	30
31						

NOVEMBER 2021
SUN	MON	TUE	WED	THU	FRI	SAT
	1	2	3	4	5	6
7	8	9	10	11	12	13
14	15	16	17	18	19	20
21	22	23	24	25	26	27
28	29	30				

DECEMBER 2021
SUN	MON	TUE	WED	THU	FRI	SAT
			1	2	3	4
5	6	7	8	9	10	11
12	13	14	15	16	17	18
19	20	21	22	23	24	25
26	27	28	29	30	31	

*MAY 2021

SUNDAY	MONDAY	TUESDAY
2	3	4
9	10	11
16	17	18
23	24	25
30	31	

NOTE

- ○
- ○
- ○
- ○
- ○
- ○
- ○
- ○
- ○
- ○

JANUARY 2021
SUN	MON	TUE	WED	THU	FRI	SAT
					1	2
3	4	5	6	7	8	9
10	11	12	13	14	15	16
17	18	19	20	21	22	23
24	25	26	27	28	29	30
31						

FEBRUARY 2021
SUN	MON	TUE	WED	THU	FRI	SAT
	1	2	3	4	5	6
7	8	9	10	11	12	13
14	15	16	17	18	19	20
21	22	23	24	25	26	27
28						

MARCH 2021
SUN	MON	TUE	WED	THU	FRI	SAT
	1	2	3	4	5	6
7	8	9	10	11	12	13
14	15	16	17	18	19	20
21	22	23	24	25	26	27
28	29	30	31			

APRIL 2021
SUN	MON	TUE	WED	THU	FRI	SAT
				1	2	3
4	5	6	7	8	9	10
11	12	13	14	15	16	17
18	19	20	21	22	23	24
25	26	27	28	29	30	

MAY 2021
SUN	MON	TUE	WED	THU	FRI	SAT
						1
2	3	4	5	6	7	8
9	10	11	12	13	14	15
16	17	18	19	20	21	22
23	24	25	26	27	28	29
30	31					

JUNE 2021
SUN	MON	TUE	WED	THU	FRI	SAT
		1	2	3	4	5
6	7	8	9	10	11	12
13	14	15	16	17	18	19
20	21	22	23	24	25	26
27	28	29	30			

WEDNESDAY	THURSDAY	FRIDAY	SATURDAY
			1
5	6	7	8
12	13	14	15
19	20	21	22
26	27	28	29

JULY 2021
SUN	MON	TUE	WED	THU	FRI	SAT
				1	2	3
4	5	6	7	8	9	10
11	12	13	14	15	16	17
18	19	20	21	22	23	24
25	26	27	28	29	30	31

AUGUST 2021
SUN	MON	TUE	WED	THU	FRI	SAT
1	2	3	4	5	6	7
8	9	10	11	12	13	14
15	16	17	18	19	20	21
22	23	24	25	26	27	28
29	30	31				

SEPTEMBER 2021
SUN	MON	TUE	WED	THU	FRI	SAT
			1	2	3	4
5	6	7	8	9	10	11
12	13	14	15	16	17	18
19	20	21	22	23	24	25
26	27	28	29	30		

OCTOBER 2021
SUN	MON	TUE	WED	THU	FRI	SAT
					1	2
3	4	5	6	7	8	9
10	11	12	13	14	15	16
17	18	19	20	21	22	23
24	25	26	27	28	29	30
31						

NOVEMBER 2021
SUN	MON	TUE	WED	THU	FRI	SAT
	1	2	3	4	5	6
7	8	9	10	11	12	13
14	15	16	17	18	19	20
21	22	23	24	25	26	27
28	29	30				

DECEMBER 2021
SUN	MON	TUE	WED	THU	FRI	SAT
			1	2	3	4
5	6	7	8	9	10	11
12	13	14	15	16	17	18
19	20	21	22	23	24	25
26	27	28	29	30	31	

*JUN 2021

NOTE

SUNDAY	MONDAY	TUESDAY
		1
6	7	8
13	14	15
20	21	22
27	28	29

JANUARY 2021
SUN	MON	TUE	WED	THU	FRI	SAT
					1	2
3	4	5	6	7	8	9
10	11	12	13	14	15	16
17	18	19	20	21	22	23
24	25	26	27	28	29	30
31						

FEBRUARY 2021
SUN	MON	TUE	WED	THU	FRI	SAT
	1	2	3	4	5	6
7	8	9	10	11	12	13
14	15	16	17	18	19	20
21	22	23	24	25	26	27
28						

MARCH 2021
SUN	MON	TUE	WED	THU	FRI	SAT
	1	2	3	4	5	6
7	8	9	10	11	12	13
14	15	16	17	18	19	20
21	22	23	24	25	26	27
28	29	30	31			

APRIL 2021
SUN	MON	TUE	WED	THU	FRI	SAT
				1	2	3
4	5	6	7	8	9	10
11	12	13	14	15	16	17
18	19	20	21	22	23	24
25	26	27	28	29	30	

MAY 2021
SUN	MON	TUE	WED	THU	FRI	SAT
						1
2	3	4	5	6	7	8
9	10	11	12	13	14	15
16	17	18	19	20	21	22
23	24	25	26	27	28	29
30	31					

JUNE 2021
SUN	MON	TUE	WED	THU	FRI	SAT
		1	2	3	4	5
6	7	8	9	10	11	12
13	14	15	16	17	18	19
20	21	22	23	24	25	26
27	28	29	30			

WEDNESDAY	THURSDAY	FRIDAY	SATURDAY
2	3	4	5
9	10	11	12
16	17	18	19
23	24	25	26
30			

JULY 2021
SUN	MON	TUE	WED	THU	FRI	SAT
				1	2	3
4	5	6	7	8	9	10
11	12	13	14	15	16	17
18	19	20	21	22	23	24
25	26	27	28	29	30	31

AUGUST 2021
SUN	MON	TUE	WED	THU	FRI	SAT
1	2	3	4	5	6	7
8	9	10	11	12	13	14
15	16	17	18	19	20	21
22	23	24	25	26	27	28
29	30	31				

SEPTEMBER 2021
SUN	MON	TUE	WED	THU	FRI	SAT
			1	2	3	4
5	6	7	8	9	10	11
12	13	14	15	16	17	18
19	20	21	22	23	24	25
26	27	28	29	30		

OCTOBER 2021
SUN	MON	TUE	WED	THU	FRI	SAT
					1	2
3	4	5	6	7	8	9
10	11	12	13	14	15	16
17	18	19	20	21	22	23
24	25	26	27	28	29	30
31						

NOVEMBER 2021
SUN	MON	TUE	WED	THU	FRI	SAT
	1	2	3	4	5	6
7	8	9	10	11	12	13
14	15	16	17	18	19	20
21	22	23	24	25	26	27
28	29	30				

DECEMBER 2021
SUN	MON	TUE	WED	THU	FRI	SAT
			1	2	3	4
5	6	7	8	9	10	11
12	13	14	15	16	17	18
19	20	21	22	23	24	25
26	27	28	29	30	31	

*JUL 2021

SUNDAY	MONDAY	TUESDAY
4	5	6
11	12	13
18	19	20
25	26	27

NOTE

JANUARY 2021	FEBRUARY 2021	MARCH 2021	APRIL 2021	MAY 2021	JUNE 2021
SUN MON TUE WED THU FRI SAT	SUN MON TUE WED THU FRI SAT	SUN MON TUE WED THU FRI SAT	SUN MON TUE WED THU FRI SAT	SUN MON TUE WED THU FRI SAT	SUN MON TUE WED THU FRI SAT
1 2	1 2 3 4 5 6	1 2 3 4 5 6	1 2 3		1 2 3 4 5
3 4 5 6 7 8 9	7 8 9 10 11 12 13	7 8 9 10 11 12 13	4 5 6 7 8 9 10	2 3 4 5 6 7 8	6 7 8 9 10 11 12
10 11 12 13 14 15 16	14 15 16 17 18 19 20	14 15 16 17 18 19 20	11 12 13 14 15 16 17	9 10 11 12 13 14 15	13 14 15 16 17 18 19
17 18 19 20 21 22 23	21 22 23 24 25 26 27	21 22 23 24 25 26 27	18 19 20 21 22 23 24	16 17 18 19 20 21 22	20 21 22 23 24 25 26
24 25 26 27 28 29 30	28	28 29 30 31	25 26 27 28 29 30	23 24 25 26 27 28 29	27 28 29 30
31				30 31	

WEDNESDAY	THURSDAY	FRIDAY	SATURDAY
	1	2	3
7	8	9	10
14	15	16	17
21	22	23	24
28	29	30	31

JULY 2021

SUN	MON	TUE	WED	THU	FRI	SAT
				1	2	3
4	5	6	7	8	9	10
11	12	13	14	15	16	17
18	19	20	21	22	23	24
25	26	27	28	29	30	31

AUGUST 2021

SUN	MON	TUE	WED	THU	FRI	SAT
1	2	3	4	5	6	7
8	9	10	11	12	13	14
15	16	17	18	19	20	21
22	23	24	25	26	27	28
29	30	31				

SEPTEMBER 2021

SUN	MON	TUE	WED	THU	FRI	SAT
			1	2	3	4
5	6	7	8	9	10	11
12	13	14	15	16	17	18
19	20	21	22	23	24	25
26	27	28	29	30		

OCTOBER 2021

SUN	MON	TUE	WED	THU	FRI	SAT
					1	2
3	4	5	6	7	8	9
10	11	12	13	14	15	16
17	18	19	20	21	22	23
24	25	26	27	28	29	30
31						

NOVEMBER 2021

SUN	MON	TUE	WED	THU	FRI	SAT
	1	2	3	4	5	6
7	8	9	10	11	12	13
14	15	16	17	18	19	20
21	22	23	24	25	26	27
28	29	30				

DECEMBER 2021

SUN	MON	TUE	WED	THU	FRI	SAT
			1	2	3	4
5	6	7	8	9	10	11
12	13	14	15	16	17	18
19	20	21	22	23	24	25
26	27	28	29	30	31	

*AUG 2021

SUNDAY	MONDAY	TUESDAY
1	2	3
8	9	10
15	16	17
22	23	24
29	30	31

NOTE

JANUARY 2021
SUN	MON	TUE	WED	THU	FRI	SAT
					1	2
3	4	5	6	7	8	9
10	11	12	13	14	15	16
17	18	19	20	21	22	23
24	25	26	27	28	29	30
31						

FEBRUARY 2021
SUN	MON	TUE	WED	THU	FRI	SAT
	1	2	3	4	5	6
7	8	9	10	11	12	13
14	15	16	17	18	19	20
21	22	23	24	25	26	27
28						

MARCH 2021
SUN	MON	TUE	WED	THU	FRI	SAT
	1	2	3	4	5	6
7	8	9	10	11	12	13
14	15	16	17	18	19	20
21	22	23	24	25	26	27
28	29	30	31			

APRIL 2021
SUN	MON	TUE	WED	THU	FRI	SAT
				1	2	3
4	5	6	7	8	9	10
11	12	13	14	15	16	17
18	19	20	21	22	23	24
25	26	27	28	29	30	

MAY 2021
SUN	MON	TUE	WED	THU	FRI	SAT
						1
2	3	4	5	6	7	8
9	10	11	12	13	14	15
16	17	18	19	20	21	22
23	24	25	26	27	28	29
30	31					

JUNE 2021
SUN	MON	TUE	WED	THU	FRI	SAT
		1	2	3	4	5
6	7	8	9	10	11	12
13	14	15	16	17	18	19
20	21	22	23	24	25	26
27	28	29	30			

WEDNESDAY	THURSDAY	FRIDAY	SATURDAY
4	5	6	7
11	12	13	14
18	19	20	21
25	26	27	28

JULY 2021

SUN	MON	TUE	WED	THU	FRI	SAT
				1	2	3
4	5	6	7	8	9	10
11	12	13	14	15	16	17
18	19	20	21	22	23	24
25	26	27	28	29	30	31

AUGUST 2021

SUN	MON	TUE	WED	THU	FRI	SAT
1	2	3	4	5	6	7
8	9	10	11	12	13	14
15	16	17	18	19	20	21
22	23	24	25	26	27	28
29	30	31				

SEPTEMBER 2021

SUN	MON	TUE	WED	THU	FRI	SAT
			1	2	3	4
5	6	7	8	9	10	11
12	13	14	15	16	17	18
19	20	21	22	23	24	25
26	27	28	29	30		

OCTOBER 2021

SUN	MON	TUE	WED	THU	FRI	SAT
					1	2
3	4	5	6	7	8	9
10	11	12	13	14	15	16
17	18	19	20	21	22	23
24	25	26	27	28	29	30
31						

NOVEMBER 2021

SUN	MON	TUE	WED	THU	FRI	SAT
	1	2	3	4	5	6
7	8	9	10	11	12	13
14	15	16	17	18	19	20
21	22	23	24	25	26	27
28	29	30				

DECEMBER 2021

SUN	MON	TUE	WED	THU	FRI	SAT
			1	2	3	4
5	6	7	8	9	10	11
12	13	14	15	16	17	18
19	20	21	22	23	24	25
26	27	28	29	30	31	

*SEP 2021

NOTE

	SUNDAY	MONDAY	TUESDAY
	5	6	7
	12	13	14
	19	20	21
	26	27	28

JANUARY 2021
SUN	MON	TUE	WED	THU	FRI	SAT
					1	2
3	4	5	6	7	8	9
10	11	12	13	14	15	16
17	18	19	20	21	22	23
24	25	26	27	28	29	30
31						

FEBRUARY 2021
SUN	MON	TUE	WED	THU	FRI	SAT
	1	2	3	4	5	6
7	8	9	10	11	12	13
14	15	16	17	18	19	20
21	22	23	24	25	26	27
28						

MARCH 2021
SUN	MON	TUE	WED	THU	FRI	SAT
	1	2	3	4	5	6
7	8	9	10	11	12	13
14	15	16	17	18	19	20
21	22	23	24	25	26	27
28	29	30	31			

APRIL 2021
SUN	MON	TUE	WED	THU	FRI	SAT
				1	2	3
4	5	6	7	8	9	10
11	12	13	14	15	16	17
18	19	20	21	22	23	24
25	26	27	28	29	30	

MAY 2021
SUN	MON	TUE	WED	THU	FRI	SAT
						1
2	3	4	5	6	7	8
9	10	11	12	13	14	15
16	17	18	19	20	21	22
23	24	25	26	27	28	29
30	31					

JUNE 2021
SUN	MON	TUE	WED	THU	FRI	SAT
		1	2	3	4	5
6	7	8	9	10	11	12
13	14	15	16	17	18	19
20	21	22	23	24	25	26
27	28	29	30			

WEDNESDAY	THURSDAY	FRIDAY	SATURDAY
1	2	3	4
8	9	10	11
15	16	17	18
22	23	24	25
29	30		

JULY 2021

SUN	MON	TUE	WED	THU	FRI	SAT
				1	2	3
4	5	6	7	8	9	10
11	12	13	14	15	16	17
18	19	20	21	22	23	24
25	26	27	28	29	30	31

AUGUST 2021

SUN	MON	TUE	WED	THU	FRI	SAT
1	2	3	4	5	6	7
8	9	10	11	12	13	14
15	16	17	18	19	20	21
22	23	24	25	26	27	28
29	30	31				

SEPTEMBER 2021

SUN	MON	TUE	WED	THU	FRI	SAT
			1	2	3	4
5	6	7	8	9	10	11
12	13	14	15	16	17	18
19	20	21	22	23	24	25
26	27	28	29	30		

OCTOBER 2021

SUN	MON	TUE	WED	THU	FRI	SAT
					1	2
3	4	5	6	7	8	9
10	11	12	13	14	15	16
17	18	19	20	21	22	23
24	25	26	27	28	29	30
31						

NOVEMBER 2021

SUN	MON	TUE	WED	THU	FRI	SAT
	1	2	3	4	5	6
7	8	9	10	11	12	13
14	15	16	17	18	19	20
21	22	23	24	25	26	27
28	29	30				

DECEMBER 2021

SUN	MON	TUE	WED	THU	FRI	SAT
			1	2	3	4
5	6	7	8	9	10	11
12	13	14	15	16	17	18
19	20	21	22	23	24	25
26	27	28	29	30	31	

*OCT 2021

SUNDAY	MONDAY	TUESDAY
3	4	5
10	11	12
17	18	19
24	25	26
31		

NOTE

- ○
- ○
- ○
- ○
- ○
- ○
- ○
- ○
- ○
- ○

JANUARY 2021
SUN	MON	TUE	WED	THU	FRI	SAT
					1	2
3	4	5	6	7	8	9
10	11	12	13	14	15	16
17	18	19	20	21	22	23
24	25	26	27	28	29	30
31						

FEBRUARY 2021
SUN	MON	TUE	WED	THU	FRI	SAT
	1	2	3	4	5	6
7	8	9	10	11	12	13
14	15	16	17	18	19	20
21	22	23	24	25	26	27
28						

MARCH 2021
SUN	MON	TUE	WED	THU	FRI	SAT
	1	2	3	4	5	6
7	8	9	10	11	12	13
14	15	16	17	18	19	20
21	22	23	24	25	26	27
28	29	30	31			

APRIL 2021
SUN	MON	TUE	WED	THU	FRI	SAT
				1	2	3
4	5	6	7	8	9	10
11	12	13	14	15	16	17
18	19	20	21	22	23	24
25	26	27	28	29	30	

MAY 2021
SUN	MON	TUE	WED	THU	FRI	SAT
						1
2	3	4	5	6	7	8
9	10	11	12	13	14	15
16	17	18	19	20	21	22
23	24	25	26	27	28	29
30	31					

JUNE 2021
SUN	MON	TUE	WED	THU	FRI	SAT
		1	2	3	4	5
6	7	8	9	10	11	12
13	14	15	16	17	18	19
20	21	22	23	24	25	26
27	28	29	30			

WEDNESDAY	THURSDAY	FRIDAY	SATURDAY
		1	2
6	7	8	9
13	14	15	16
20	21	22	23
27	28	29	30

JULY 2021
SUN	MON	TUE	WED	THU	FRI	SAT
				1	2	3
4	5	6	7	8	9	10
11	12	13	14	15	16	17
18	19	20	21	22	23	24
25	26	27	28	29	30	31

AUGUST 2021
SUN	MON	TUE	WED	THU	FRI	SAT
1	2	3	4	5	6	7
8	9	10	11	12	13	14
15	16	17	18	19	20	21
22	23	24	25	26	27	28
29	30	31				

SEPTEMBER 2021
SUN	MON	TUE	WED	THU	FRI	SAT
			1	2	3	4
5	6	7	8	9	10	11
12	13	14	15	16	17	18
19	20	21	22	23	24	25
26	27	28	29	30		

OCTOBER 2021
SUN	MON	TUE	WED	THU	FRI	SAT
					1	2
3	4	5	6	7	8	9
10	11	12	13	14	15	16
17	18	19	20	21	22	23
24	25	26	27	28	29	30
31						

NOVEMBER 2021
SUN	MON	TUE	WED	THU	FRI	SAT
	1	2	3	4	5	6
7	8	9	10	11	12	13
14	15	16	17	18	19	20
21	22	23	24	25	26	27
28	29	30				

DECEMBER 2021
SUN	MON	TUE	WED	THU	FRI	SAT
			1	2	3	4
5	6	7	8	9	10	11
12	13	14	15	16	17	18
19	20	21	22	23	24	25
26	27	28	29	30	31	

*NOV 2021

NOTE

SUNDAY	MONDAY	TUESDAY
	1	2
7	8	9
14	15	16
21	22	23
28	29	30

JANUARY 2021
MON	TUE	WED	THU	FRI	SAT
				1	2
4	5	6	7	8	9
11	12	13	14	15	16
18	19	20	21	22	23
25	26	27	28	29	30

FEBRUARY 2021
SUN	MON	TUE	WED	THU	FRI	SAT
	1	2	3	4	5	6
7	8	9	10	11	12	13
14	15	16	17	18	19	20
21	22	23	24	25	26	27
28						

MARCH 2021
SUN	MON	TUE	WED	THU	FRI	SAT
	1	2	3	4	5	6
7	8	9	10	11	12	13
14	15	16	17	18	19	20
21	22	23	24	25	26	27
28	29	30	31			

APRIL 2021
SUN	MON	TUE	WED	THU	FRI	SAT
				1	2	3
4	5	6	7	8	9	10
11	12	13	14	15	16	17
18	19	20	21	22	23	24
25	26	27	28	29	30	

MAY 2021
SUN	MON	TUE	WED	THU	FRI	SAT
						1
2	3	4	5	6	7	8
9	10	11	12	13	14	15
16	17	18	19	20	21	22
23	24	25	26	27	28	29
30	31					

JUNE 2021
SUN	MON	TUE	WED	THU	FRI	SAT
		1	2	3	4	5
6	7	8	9	10	11	12
13	14	15	16	17	18	19
20	21	22	23	24	25	26
27	28	29	30			

WEDNESDAY	THURSDAY	FRIDAY	SATURDAY
3	4	5	6
10	11	12	13
17	18	19	20
24	25	26	27

JULY 2021
SUN	MON	TUE	WED	THU	FRI	SAT
				1	2	3
4	5	6	7	8	9	10
11	12	13	14	15	16	17
18	19	20	21	22	23	24
25	26	27	28	29	30	31

AUGUST 2021
SUN	MON	TUE	WED	THU	FRI	SAT
1	2	3	4	5	6	7
8	9	10	11	12	13	14
15	16	17	18	19	20	21
22	23	24	25	26	27	28
29	30	31				

SEPTEMBER 2021
SUN	MON	TUE	WED	THU	FRI	SAT
			1	2	3	4
5	6	7	8	9	10	11
12	13	14	15	16	17	18
19	20	21	22	23	24	25
26	27	28	29	30		

OCTOBER 2021
SUN	MON	TUE	WED	THU	FRI	SAT
					1	2
3	4	5	6	7	8	9
10	11	12	13	14	15	16
17	18	19	20	21	22	23
24	25	26	27	28	29	30
31						

NOVEMBER 2021
SUN	MON	TUE	WED	THU	FRI	SAT
	1	2	3	4	5	6
7	8	9	10	11	12	13
14	15	16	17	18	19	20
21	22	23	24	25	26	27
28	29	30				

DECEMBER 2021
SUN	MON	TUE	WED	THU	FRI	SAT
			1	2	3	4
5	6	7	8	9	10	11
12	13	14	15	16	17	18
19	20	21	22	23	24	25
26	27	28	29	30	31	

SUNDAY	MONDAY	TUESDAY
5	6	7
12	13	14
19	20	21
26	27	28

NOTE

- ○
- ○
- ○
- ○
- ○
- ○
- ○
- ○
- ○
- ○

JANUARY 2021
SUN	MON	TUE	WED	THU	FRI	SAT
					1	2
3	4	5	6	7	8	9
10	11	12	13	14	15	16
17	18	19	20	21	22	23
24	25	26	27	28	29	30
31						

FEBRUARY 2021
SUN	MON	TUE	WED	THU	FRI	SAT
	1	2	3	4	5	6
7	8	9	10	11	12	13
14	15	16	17	18	19	20
21	22	23	24	25	26	27
28						

MARCH 2021
SUN	MON	TUE	WED	THU	FRI	SAT
	1	2	3	4	5	6
7	8	9	10	11	12	13
14	15	16	17	18	19	20
21	22	23	24	25	26	27
28	29	30	31			

APRIL 2021
SUN	MON	TUE	WED	THU	FRI	SAT
				1	2	3
4	5	6	7	8	9	10
11	12	13	14	15	16	17
18	19	20	21	22	23	24
25	26	27	28	29	30	

MAY 2021
SUN	MON	TUE	WED	THU	FRI	SAT
						1
2	3	4	5	6	7	8
9	10	11	12	13	14	15
16	17	18	19	20	21	22
23	24	25	26	27	28	29
30	31					

JUNE 2021
SUN	MON	TUE	WED	THU	FRI	SAT
		1	2	3	4	5
6	7	8	9	10	11	12
13	14	15	16	17	18	19
20	21	22	23	24	25	26
27	28	29	30			

WEDNESDAY	THURSDAY	FRIDAY	SATURDAY
1	2	3	4
8	9	10	11
15	16	17	18
22	23	24	25
29	30	31	

JULY 2021

SUN	MON	TUE	WED	THU	FRI	SAT
				1	2	3
4	5	6	7	8	9	10
11	12	13	14	15	16	17
18	19	20	21	22	23	24
25	26	27	28	29	30	31

AUGUST 2021

SUN	MON	TUE	WED	THU	FRI	SAT
1	2	3	4	5	6	7
8	9	10	11	12	13	14
15	16	17	18	19	20	21
22	23	24	25	26	27	28
29	30	31				

SEPTEMBER 2021

SUN	MON	TUE	WED	THU	FRI	SAT
			1	2	3	4
5	6	7	8	9	10	11
12	13	14	15	16	17	18
19	20	21	22	23	24	25
26	27	28	29	30		

OCTOBER 2021

SUN	MON	TUE	WED	THU	FRI	SAT
					1	2
3	4	5	6	7	8	9
10	11	12	13	14	15	16
17	18	19	20	21	22	23
24	25	26	27	28	29	30
31						

NOVEMBER 2021

SUN	MON	TUE	WED	THU	FRI	SAT
	1	2	3	4	5	6
7	8	9	10	11	12	13
14	15	16	17	18	19	20
21	22	23	24	25	26	27
28	29	30				

DECEMBER 2021

SUN	MON	TUE	WED	THU	FRI	SAT
			1	2	3	4
5	6	7	8	9	10	11
12	13	14	15	16	17	18
19	20	21	22	23	24	25
26	27	28	29	30	31	

2022

JANUARY
SUN	MON	TUE	WED	THU	FRI	SAT
						1
2	3	4	5	6	7	8
9	10	11	12	13	14	15
16	17	18	19	20	21	22
23	24	25	26	27	28	29
30	31					

FEBRUARY
SUN	MON	TUE	WED	THU	FRI	SAT
		1	2	3	4	5
6	7	8	9	10	11	12
13	14	15	16	17	18	19
20	21	22	23	24	25	26
27	28					

MARCH
SUN	MON	TUE	WED	THU	FRI	SAT
		1	2	3	4	5
6	7	8	9	10	11	12
13	14	15	16	17	18	19
20	21	22	23	24	25	26
27	28	29	30	31		

APRIL
SUN	MON	TUE	WED	THU	FRI	SAT
					1	2
3	4	5	6	7	8	9
10	11	12	13	14	15	16
17	18	19	20	21	22	23
24	25	26	27	28	29	30

MAY
SUN	MON	TUE	WED	THU	FRI	SAT
1	2	3	4	5	6	7
8	9	10	11	12	13	14
15	16	17	18	19	20	21
22	23	24	25	26	27	28
29	30	31				

JUNE
SUN	MON	TUE	WED	THU	FRI	SAT
			1	2	3	4
5	6	7	8	9	10	11
12	13	14	15	16	17	18
19	20	21	22	23	24	25
26	27	28	29	30		

JULY
SUN	MON	TUE	WED	THU	FRI	SAT
					1	2
3	4	5	6	7	8	9
10	11	12	13	14	15	16
17	18	19	20	21	22	23
24	25	26	27	28	29	30
31						

AUGUST
SUN	MON	TUE	WED	THU	FRI	SAT
	1	2	3	4	5	6
7	8	9	10	11	12	13
14	15	16	17	18	19	20
21	22	23	24	25	26	27
28	29	30	31			

SEPTEMBER
SUN	MON	TUE	WED	THU	FRI	SAT
				1	2	3
4	5	6	7	8	9	10
11	12	13	14	15	16	17
18	19	20	21	22	23	24
25	26	27	28	29	30	

OCTOBER
SUN	MON	TUE	WED	THU	FRI	SAT
						1
2	3	4	5	6	7	8
9	10	11	12	13	14	15
16	17	18	19	20	21	22
23	24	25	26	27	28	29
30	31					

NOVEMBER
SUN	MON	TUE	WED	THU	FRI	SAT
		1	2	3	4	5
6	7	8	9	10	11	12
13	14	15	16	17	18	19
20	21	22	23	24	25	26
27	28	29	30			

DECEMBER
SUN	MON	TUE	WED	THU	FRI	SAT
				1	2	3
4	5	6	7	8	9	10
11	12	13	14	15	16	17
18	19	20	21	22	23	24
25	26	27	28	29	30	

*JAN 2022

SUNDAY	MONDAY	TUESDAY
2	3	4
9	10	11
16	17	18
23	24	25
30	31	

NOTE

○
○
○
○
○
○
○
○
○
○

JANUARY 2021

Sun	Mon	Tue	Wed	Thu	Fri	Sat
						1
2	3	4	5	6	7	8
9	10	11	12	13	14	15
16	17	18	19	20	21	22
23	24	25	26	27	28	29
30	31					

FEBRUARY 2022

Sun	Mon	Tue	Wed	Thu	Fri	Sat
		1	2	3	4	5
6	7	8	9	10	11	12
13	14	15	16	17	18	19
20	21	22	23	24	25	26
27	28					

MARCH 2022

Sun	Mon	Tue	Wed	Thu	Fri	Sat
		1	2	3	4	5
6	7	8	9	10	11	12
13	14	15	16	17	18	19
20	21	22	23	24	25	26
27	28	29	30	31		

APRIL 2022

Sun	Mon	Tue	Wed	Thu	Fri	Sat
					1	2
3	4	5	6	7	8	9
10	11	12	13	14	15	16
17	18	19	20	21	22	23
24	25	26	27	28	29	30

MAY 2022

Sun	Mon	Tue	Wed	Thu	Fri	Sat
1	2	3	4	5	6	7
8	9	10	11	12	13	14
15	16	17	18	19	20	21
22	23	24	25	26	27	28
29	30	31				

JUNE 2022

Sun	Mon	Tue	Wed	Thu	Fri	Sat
			1	2	3	4
5	6	7	8	9	10	11
12	13	14	15	16	17	18
19	20	21	22	23	24	25
26	27	28	29	30		

WEDNESDAY	THURSDAY	FRIDAY	SATURDAY
			1
5	6	7	8
12	13	14	15
19	20	21	22
26	27	28	29

JULY 2022
SUN	MON	TUE	WED	THU	FRI	SAT
					1	2
3	4	5	6	7	8	9
10	11	12	13	14	15	16
17	18	19	20	21	22	23
24	25	26	27	28	29	30
31						

AUGUST 2022
SUN	MON	TUE	WED	THU	FRI	SAT
	1	2	3	4	5	6
7	8	9	10	11	12	13
14	15	16	17	18	19	20
21	22	23	24	25	26	27
28	29	30	31			

SEPTEMBER 2022
SUN	MON	TUE	WED	THU	FRI	SAT
				1	2	3
4	5	6	7	8	9	10
11	12	13	14	15	16	17
18	19	20	21	22	23	24
25	26	27	28	29	30	

OCTOBER 2022
SUN	MON	TUE	WED	THU	FRI	SAT
						1
2	3	4	5	6	7	8
9	10	11	12	13	14	15
16	17	18	19	20	21	22
23	24	25	26	27	28	29
30						

NOVEMBER 2022
SUN	MON	TUE	WED	THU	FRI	SAT
		1	2	3	4	5
6	7	8	9	10	11	12
13	14	15	16	17	18	19
20	21	22	23	24	25	26
27	28	29	30			

DECEMBER 2022
SUN	MON	TUE	WED	THU	FRI	SAT
				1	2	3
4	5	6	7	8	9	10
11	12	13	14	15	16	17
18	19	20	21	22	23	24
25	26	27	28	29	30	

*FEB 2022

NOTE

SUNDAY	MONDAY	TUESDAY
		1
6	**7**	**8**
13	**14**	**15**
20	**21**	**22**
27	**28**	

JANUARY 2021
SUN	MON	TUE	WED	THU	FRI	SAT
					1	2
3	4	5	6	7	8	9
10	11	12	13	14	15	16
17	18	19	20	21	22	23
24	25	26	27	28	29	30
31						

FEBRUARY 2022
SUN	MON	TUE	WED	THU	FRI	SAT
		1	2	3	4	5
6	7	8	9	10	11	12
13	14	15	16	17	18	19
20	21	22	23	24	25	26
27	28					

MARCH 2022
SUN	MON	TUE	WED	THU	FRI	SAT
		1	2	3	4	5
6	7	8	9	10	11	12
13	14	15	16	17	18	19
20	21	22	23	24	25	26
27	28	29	30	31		

APRIL 2022
SUN	MON	TUE	WED	THU	FRI	SAT
					1	2
3	4	5	6	7	8	9
10	11	12	13	14	15	16
17	18	19	20	21	22	23
24	25	26	27	28	29	30

MAY 2022
SUN	MON	TUE	WED	THU	FRI	SAT
1	2	3	4	5	6	7
8	9	10	11	12	13	14
15	16	17	18	19	20	21
22	23	24	25	26	27	28
29	30	31				

JUNE 2022
SUN	MON	TUE	WED	THU	FRI	SAT
			1	2	3	4
5	6	7	8	9	10	11
12	13	14	15	16	17	18
19	20	21	22	23	24	25
26	27	28	29	30		

WEDNESDAY	THURSDAY	FRIDAY	SATURDAY
2	3	4	5
9	10	11	12
16	17	18	19
23	24	25	26

JULY 2022

SUN	MON	TUE	WED	THU	FRI	SAT
					1	2
3	4	5	6	7	8	9
10	11	12	13	14	15	16
17	18	19	20	21	22	23
24	25	26	27	28	29	30
31						

AUGUST 2022

SUN	MON	TUE	WED	THU	FRI	SAT
	1	2	3	4	5	6
7	8	9	10	11	12	13
14	15	16	17	18	19	20
21	22	23	24	25	26	27
28	29	30	31			

SEPTEMBER 2022

SUN	MON	TUE	WED	THU	FRI	SAT
				1	2	3
4	5	6	7	8	9	10
11	12	13	14	15	16	17
18	19	20	21	22	23	24
25	26	27	28	29	30	

OCTOBER 2022

SUN	MON	TUE	WED	THU	FRI	SAT
						1
2	3	4	5	6	7	8
9	10	11	12	13	14	15
16	17	18	19	20	21	22
23	24	25	26	27	28	29
30						

NOVEMBER 2022

SUN	MON	TUE	WED	THU	FRI	SAT
		1	2	3	4	5
6	7	8	9	10	11	12
13	14	15	16	17	18	19
20	21	22	23	24	25	26
27	28	29	30			

DECEMBER 2022

SUN	MON	TUE	WED	THU	FRI	SAT
				1	2	3
4	5	6	7	8	9	10
11	12	13	14	15	16	17
18	19	20	21	22	23	24
25	26	27	28	29	30	

*MAR 2022

NOTE

SUNDAY	MONDAY	TUESDAY
		1
6	7	8
13	14	15
20	21	22
27	28	29

JANUARY 2021
SUN	MON	TUE	WED	THU	FRI	SAT
					1	2
3	4	5	6	7	8	9
10	11	12	13	14	15	16
17	18	19	20	21	22	23
24	25	26	27	28	29	30
31						

FEBRUARY 2022
SUN	MON	TUE	WED	THU	FRI	SAT
		1	2	3	4	5
6	7	8	9	10	11	12
13	14	15	16	17	18	19
20	21	22	23	24	25	26
27	28					

MARCH 2022
SUN	MON	TUE	WED	THU	FRI	SAT
		1	2	3	4	5
6	7	8	9	10	11	12
13	14	15	16	17	18	19
20	21	22	23	24	25	26
27	28	29	30	31		

APRIL 2022
SUN	MON	TUE	WED	THU	FRI	SAT
					1	2
3	4	5	6	7	8	9
10	11	12	13	14	15	16
17	18	19	20	21	22	23
24	25	26	27	28	29	30

MAY 2022
SUN	MON	TUE	WED	THU	FRI	SAT
1	2	3	4	5	6	7
8	9	10	11	12	13	14
15	16	17	18	19	20	21
22	23	24	25	26	27	28
29	30	31				

JUNE 2022
SUN	MON	TUE	WED	THU	FRI	SAT
			1	2	3	4
5	6	7	8	9	10	11
12	13	14	15	16	17	18
19	20	21	22	23	24	25
26	27	28	29	30		

WEDNESDAY	THURSDAY	FRIDAY	SATURDAY
2	3	4	5
9	10	11	12
16	17	18	19
23	24	25	26
30	31		

JULY 2022
SUN	MON	TUE	WED	THU	FRI	SAT
					1	2
3	4	5	6	7	8	9
10	11	12	13	14	15	16
17	18	19	20	21	22	23
24	25	26	27	28	29	30
31						

AUGUST 2022
SUN	MON	TUE	WED	THU	FRI	SAT
	1	2	3	4	5	6
7	8	9	10	11	12	13
14	15	16	17	18	19	20
21	22	23	24	25	26	27
28	29	30	31			

SEPTEMBER 2022
SUN	MON	TUE	WED	THU	FRI	SAT
				1	2	3
4	5	6	7	8	9	10
11	12	13	14	15	16	17
18	19	20	21	22	23	24
25	26	27	28	29	30	

OCTOBER 2022
SUN	MON	TUE	WED	THU	FRI	SAT
						1
2	3	4	5	6	7	8
9	10	11	12	13	14	15
16	17	18	19	20	21	22
23	24	25	26	27	28	29
30						

NOVEMBER 2022
SUN	MON	TUE	WED	THU	FRI	SAT
		1	2	3	4	5
6	7	8	9	10	11	12
13	14	15	16	17	18	19
20	21	22	23	24	25	26
27	28	29	30			

DECEMBER 2022
SUN	MON	TUE	WED	THU	FRI	SAT
				1	2	3
4	5	6	7	8	9	10
11	12	13	14	15	16	17
18	19	20	21	22	23	24
25	26	27	28	29	30	31

NOTE

SUNDAY	MONDAY	TUESDAY
3	4	5
10	11	12
17	18	19
24	25	26

JANUARY 2021

SUN	MON	TUE	WED	THU	FRI	SAT
					1	2
3	4	5	6	7	8	9
10	11	12	13	14	15	16
17	18	19	20	21	22	23
24	25	26	27	28	29	30
31						

FEBRUARY 2022

SUN	MON	TUE	WED	THU	FRI	SAT
		1	2	3	4	5
6	7	8	9	10	11	12
13	14	15	16	17	18	19
20	21	22	23	24	25	26
27	28					

MARCH 2022

SUN	MON	TUE	WED	THU	FRI	SAT
		1	2	3	4	5
6	7	8	9	10	11	12
13	14	15	16	17	18	19
20	21	22	23	24	25	26
27	28	29	30	31		

APRIL 2022

SUN	MON	TUE	WED	THU	FRI	SAT
					1	2
3	4	5	6	7	8	9
10	11	12	13	14	15	16
17	18	19	20	21	22	23
24	25	26	27	28	29	30

MAY 2022

SUN	MON	TUE	WED	THU	FRI	SAT
1	2	3	4	5	6	7
8	9	10	11	12	13	14
15	16	17	18	19	20	21
22	23	24	25	26	27	28
29	30	31				

JUNE 2022

SUN	MON	TUE	WED	THU	FRI	SAT
			1	2	3	4
5	6	7	8	9	10	11
12	13	14	15	16	17	18
19	20	21	22	23	24	25
26	27	28	29	30		

WEDNESDAY	THURSDAY	FRIDAY	SATURDAY
		1	2
6	7	8	9
13	14	15	16
20	21	22	23
27	28	29	30

JULY 2022
SUN	MON	TUE	WED	THU	FRI	SAT
					1	2
3	4	5	6	7	8	9
10	11	12	13	14	15	16
17	18	19	20	21	22	23
24	25	26	27	28	29	30
31						

AUGUST 2022
SUN	MON	TUE	WED	THU	FRI	SAT
	1	2	3	4	5	6
7	8	9	10	11	12	13
14	15	16	17	18	19	20
21	22	23	24	25	26	27
28	29	30	31			

SEPTEMBER 2022
SUN	MON	TUE	WED	THU	FRI	SAT
				1	2	3
4	5	6	7	8	9	10
11	12	13	14	15	16	17
18	19	20	21	22	23	24
25	26	27	28	29	30	

OCTOBER 2022
SUN	MON	TUE	WED	THU	FRI	SAT
						1
2	3	4	5	6	7	8
9	10	11	12	13	14	15
16	17	18	19	20	21	22
23	24	25	26	27	28	29
30						

NOVEMBER 2022
SUN	MON	TUE	WED	THU	FRI	SAT
		1	2	3	4	5
6	7	8	9	10	11	12
13	14	15	16	17	18	19
20	21	22	23	24	25	26
27	28	29	30			

DECEMBER 2022
SUN	MON	TUE	WED	THU	FRI	SAT
				1	2	3
4	5	6	7	8	9	10
11	12	13	14	15	16	17
18	19	20	21	22	23	24
25	26	27	28	29	30	

*MAY 2022

SUNDAY	MONDAY	TUESDAY
1	2	3
8	9	10
15	16	17
22	23	24
29	30	31

NOTE

○
○
○
○
○
○
○
○
○
○

JANUARY 2021
SUN	MON	TUE	WED	THU	FRI	SAT
						1
2	3	4	5	6	7	8
9	10	11	12	13	14	15
16	17	18	19	20	21	22
23	24	25	26	27	28	29
30	31					

FEBRUARY 2022
SUN	MON	TUE	WED	THU	FRI	SAT
		1	2	3	4	5
6	7	8	9	10	11	12
13	14	15	16	17	18	19
20	21	22	23	24	25	26
27	28					

MARCH 2022
SUN	MON	TUE	WED	THU	FRI	SAT
		1	2	3	4	5
6	7	8	9	10	11	12
13	14	15	16	17	18	19
20	21	22	23	24	25	26
27	28	29	30	31		

APRIL 2022
SUN	MON	TUE	WED	THU	FRI	SAT
					1	2
3	4	5	6	7	8	9
10	11	12	13	14	15	16
17	18	19	20	21	22	23
24	25	26	27	28	29	30

MAY 2022
SUN	MON	TUE	WED	THU	FRI	SAT
1	2	3	4	5	6	7
8	9	10	11	12	13	14
15	16	17	18	19	20	21
22	23	24	25	26	27	28
29	30	31				

JUNE 2022
SUN	MON	TUE	WED	THU	FRI	SAT
			1	2	3	4
5	6	7	8	9	10	11
12	13	14	15	16	17	18
19	20	21	22	23	24	25
26	27	28	29	30		

WEDNESDAY	THURSDAY	FRIDAY	SATURDAY
4	5	6	7
11	12	13	14
18	19	20	21
25	26	27	28

JULY 2022

SUN	MON	TUE	WED	THU	FRI	SAT
					1	2
3	4	5	6	7	8	9
10	11	12	13	14	15	16
17	18	19	20	21	22	23
24	25	26	27	28	29	30
31						

AUGUST 2022

SUN	MON	TUE	WED	THU	FRI	SAT
	1	2	3	4	5	6
7	8	9	10	11	12	13
14	15	16	17	18	19	20
21	22	23	24	25	26	27
28	29	30	31			

SEPTEMBER 2022

SUN	MON	TUE	WED	THU	FRI	SAT
				1	2	3
4	5	6	7	8	9	10
11	12	13	14	15	16	17
18	19	20	21	22	23	24
25	26	27	28	29	30	

OCTOBER 2022

SUN	MON	TUE	WED	THU	FRI	SAT
						1
2	3	4	5	6	7	8
9	10	11	12	13	14	15
16	17	18	19	20	21	22
23	24	25	26	27	28	29
30						

NOVEMBER 2022

SUN	MON	TUE	WED	THU	FRI	SAT
		1	2	3	4	5
6	7	8	9	10	11	12
13	14	15	16	17	18	19
20	21	22	23	24	25	26
27	28	29	30			

DECEMBER 2022

SUN	MON	TUE	WED	THU	FRI	SAT
				1	2	3
4	5	6	7	8	9	10
11	12	13	14	15	16	17
18	19	20	21	22	23	24
25	26	27	28	29	30	31

*JUN 2022

SUNDAY	MONDAY	TUESDAY
5	6	7
12	13	14
19	20	21
26	27	28

NOTE

- ○
- ○
- ○
- ○
- ○
- ○
- ○
- ○
- ○
- ○

JANUARY 2021
SUN	MON	TUE	WED	THU	FRI	SAT
					1	
2	3	4	5	6	7	8
9	10	11	12	13	14	15
16	17	18	19	20	21	22
23	24	25	26	27	28	29
30	31					

FEBRUARY 2022
SUN	MON	TUE	WED	THU	FRI	SAT
		1	2	3	4	5
6	7	8	9	10	11	12
13	14	15	16	17	18	19
20	21	22	23	24	25	26
27	28					

MARCH 2022
SUN	MON	TUE	WED	THU	FRI	SAT
		1	2	3	4	5
6	7	8	9	10	11	12
13	14	15	16	17	18	19
20	21	22	23	24	25	26
27	28	29	30	31		

APRIL 2022
SUN	MON	TUE	WED	THU	FRI	SAT
					1	2
3	4	5	6	7	8	9
10	11	12	13	14	15	16
17	18	19	20	21	22	23
24	25	26	27	28	29	30

MAY 2022
SUN	MON	TUE	WED	THU	FRI	SAT
1	2	3	4	5	6	7
8	9	10	11	12	13	14
15	16	17	18	19	20	21
22	23	24	25	26	27	28
29	30	31				

JUNE 2022
SUN	MON	TUE	WED	THU	FRI	SAT
			1	2	3	4
5	6	7	8	9	10	11
12	13	14	15	16	17	18
19	20	21	22	23	24	25
26	27	28	29	30		

WEDNESDAY	THURSDAY	FRIDAY	SATURDAY
1	2	3	4
8	9	10	11
15	16	17	18
22	23	24	25
29	30		

JULY 2022
SUN	MON	TUE	WED	THU	FRI	SAT
					1	2
3	4	5	6	7	8	9
10	11	12	13	14	15	16
17	18	19	20	21	22	23
24	25	26	27	28	29	30
31						

AUGUST 2022
SUN	MON	TUE	WED	THU	FRI	SAT
	1	2	3	4	5	6
7	8	9	10	11	12	13
14	15	16	17	18	19	20
21	22	23	24	25	26	27
28	29	30	31			

SEPTEMBER 2022
SUN	MON	TUE	WED	THU	FRI	SAT
				1	2	3
4	5	6	7	8	9	10
11	12	13	14	15	16	17
18	19	20	21	22	23	24
25	26	27	28	29	30	

OCTOBER 2022
SUN	MON	TUE	WED	THU	FRI	SAT
						1
2	3	4	5	6	7	8
9	10	11	12	13	14	15
16	17	18	19	20	21	22
23	24	25	26	27	28	29
30						

NOVEMBER 2022
SUN	MON	TUE	WED	THU	FRI	SAT
		1	2	3	4	5
6	7	8	9	10	11	12
13	14	15	16	17	18	19
20	21	22	23	24	25	26
27	28	29	30			

DECEMBER 2022
SUN	MON	TUE	WED	THU	FRI	SAT
				1	2	3
4	5	6	7	8	9	10
11	12	13	14	15	16	17
18	19	20	21	22	23	24
25	26	27	28	29	30	

*JUL 2022

SUNDAY	MONDAY	TUESDAY
3	4	5
10	11	12
17	18	19
24	25	26
31		

NOTE

- ○
- ○
- ○
- ○
- ○
- ○
- ○
- ○
- ○
- ○

JANUARY 2021
SUN	MON	TUE	WED	THU	FRI	SAT
					1	2
3	4	5	6	7	8	9
10	11	12	13	14	15	16
17	18	19	20	21	22	23
24	25	26	27	28	29	30
31						

FEBRUARY 2022
SUN	MON	TUE	WED	THU	FRI	SAT
		1	2	3	4	5
6	7	8	9	10	11	12
13	14	15	16	17	18	19
20	21	22	23	24	25	26
27	28					

MARCH 2022
SUN	MON	TUE	WED	THU	FRI	SAT
		1	2	3	4	5
6	7	8	9	10	11	12
13	14	15	16	17	18	19
20	21	22	23	24	25	26
27	28	29	30	31		

APRIL 2022
SUN	MON	TUE	WED	THU	FRI	SAT
					1	2
3	4	5	6	7	8	9
10	11	12	13	14	15	16
17	18	19	20	21	22	23
24	25	26	27	28	29	30

MAY 2022
SUN	MON	TUE	WED	THU	FRI	SAT
1	2	3	4	5	6	7
8	9	10	11	12	13	14
15	16	17	18	19	20	21
22	23	24	25	26	27	28
29	30	31				

JUNE 2022
SUN	MON	TUE	WED	THU	FRI	SAT
			1	2	3	4
5	6	7	8	9	10	11
12	13	14	15	16	17	18
19	20	21	22	23	24	25
26	27	28	29	30		

WEDNESDAY	THURSDAY	FRIDAY	SATURDAY
		1	2
6	7	8	9
13	14	15	16
20	21	22	23
27	28	29	30

JULY 2022
SUN	MON	TUE	WED	THU	FRI	SAT
					1	2
3	4	5	6	7	8	9
10	11	12	13	14	15	16
17	18	19	20	21	22	23
24	25	26	27	28	29	30
31						

AUGUST 2022
SUN	MON	TUE	WED	THU	FRI	SAT
	1	2	3	4	5	6
7	8	9	10	11	12	13
14	15	16	17	18	19	20
21	22	23	24	25	26	27
28	29	30	31			

SEPTEMBER 2022
SUN	MON	TUE	WED	THU	FRI	SAT
				1	2	3
4	5	6	7	8	9	10
11	12	13	14	15	16	17
18	19	20	21	22	23	24
25	26	27	28	29	30	

OCTOBER 2022
SUN	MON	TUE	WED	THU	FRI	SAT
						1
2	3	4	5	6	7	8
9	10	11	12	13	14	15
16	17	18	19	20	21	22
23	24	25	26	27	28	29
30						

NOVEMBER 2022
SUN	MON	TUE	WED	THU	FRI	SAT
		1	2	3	4	5
6	7	8	9	10	11	12
13	14	15	16	17	18	19
20	21	22	23	24	25	26
27	28	29	30			

DECEMBER 2022
SUN	MON	TUE	WED	THU	FRI	SAT
				1	2	3
4	5	6	7	8	9	10
11	12	13	14	15	16	17
18	19	20	21	22	23	24
25	26	27	28	29	30	

NOTE

SUNDAY	MONDAY	TUESDAY
	1	2
7	8	9
14	15	16
21	22	23
28	29	30

- ○
- ○
- ○
- ○
- ○
- ○
- ○
- ○
- ○
- ○

JANUARY 2021
SUN	MON	TUE	WED	THU	FRI	SAT
					1
2	3	4	5	6	7	8
9	10	11	12	13	14	15
16	17	18	19	20	21	22
23	24	25	26	27	28	29
30	31

FEBRUARY 2022
SUN	MON	TUE	WED	THU	FRI	SAT
		1	2	3	4	5
6	7	8	9	10	11	12
13	14	15	16	17	18	19
20	21	22	23	24	25	26
27	28

MARCH 2022
SUN	MON	TUE	WED	THU	FRI	SAT
		1	2	3	4	5
6	7	8	9	10	11	12
13	14	15	16	17	18	19
20	21	22	23	24	25	26
27	28	29	30	31

APRIL 2022
SUN	MON	TUE	WED	THU	FRI	SAT
					1	2
3	4	5	6	7	8	9
10	11	12	13	14	15	16
17	18	19	20	21	22	23
24	25	26	27	28	29	30

MAY 2022
SUN	MON	TUE	WED	THU	FRI	SAT
1	2	3	4	5	6	7
8	9	10	11	12	13	14
15	16	17	18	19	20	21
22	23	24	25	26	27	28
29	30	31

JUNE 2022
SUN	MON	TUE	WED	THU	FRI	SAT
			1	2	3	4
5	6	7	8	9	10	11
12	13	14	15	16	17	18
19	20	21	22	23	24	25
26	27	28	29	30

WEDNESDAY	THURSDAY	FRIDAY	SATURDAY
3	4	5	6
10	11	12	13
17	18	19	20
24	25	26	27
31			

JULY 2022

SUN	MON	TUE	WED	THU	FRI	SAT
					1	2
3	4	5	6	7	8	9
10	11	12	13	14	15	16
17	18	19	20	21	22	23
24	25	26	27	28	29	30
31						

AUGUST 2022

SUN	MON	TUE	WED	THU	FRI	SAT
	1	2	3	4	5	6
7	8	9	10	11	12	13
14	15	16	17	18	19	20
21	22	23	24	25	26	27
28	29	30	31			

SEPTEMBER 2022

SUN	MON	TUE	WED	THU	FRI	SAT
				1	2	3
4	5	6	7	8	9	10
11	12	13	14	15	16	17
18	19	20	21	22	23	24
25	26	27	28	29	30	

OCTOBER 2022

SUN	MON	TUE	WED	THU	FRI	SAT
						1
2	3	4	5	6	7	8
9	10	11	12	13	14	15
16	17	18	19	20	21	22
23	24	25	26	27	28	29
30						

NOVEMBER 2022

SUN	MON	TUE	WED	THU	FRI	SAT
		1	2	3	4	5
6	7	8	9	10	11	12
13	14	15	16	17	18	19
20	21	22	23	24	25	26
27	28	29	30			

DECEMBER 2022

SUN	MON	TUE	WED	THU	FRI	SAT
				1	2	3
4	5	6	7	8	9	10
11	12	13	14	15	16	17
18	19	20	21	22	23	24
25	26	27	28	29	30	

*SEP 2022

SUNDAY	MONDAY	TUESDAY
4	5	6
11	12	13
18	19	20
25	26	27

NOTE

- ○
- ○
- ○
- ○
- ○
- ○
- ○
- ○
- ○
- ○

JANUARY 2021						
SUN	MON	TUE	WED	THU	FRI	SAT
						1
2	3	4	5	6	7	8
9	10	11	12	13	14	15
16	17	18	19	20	21	22
23	24	25	26	27	28	29
30	31					

FEBRUARY 2022						
SUN	MON	TUE	WED	THU	FRI	SAT
		1	2	3	4	5
6	7	8	9	10	11	12
13	14	15	16	17	18	19
20	21	22	23	24	25	26
27	28					

MARCH 2022						
SUN	MON	TUE	WED	THU	FRI	SAT
		1	2	3	4	5
6	7	8	9	10	11	12
13	14	15	16	17	18	19
20	21	22	23	24	25	26
27	28	29	30	31		

APRIL 2022						
SUN	MON	TUE	WED	THU	FRI	SAT
					1	2
3	4	5	6	7	8	9
10	11	12	13	14	15	16
17	18	19	20	21	22	23
24	25	26	27	28	29	30

MAY 2022						
SUN	MON	TUE	WED	THU	FRI	SAT
1	2	3	4	5	6	7
8	9	10	11	12	13	14
15	16	17	18	19	20	21
22	23	24	25	26	27	28
29	30	31				

JUNE 2022						
SUN	MON	TUE	WED	THU	FRI	SAT
			1	2	3	4
5	6	7	8	9	10	11
12	13	14	15	16	17	18
19	20	21	22	23	24	25
26	27	28	29	30		

WEDNESDAY	THURSDAY	FRIDAY	SATURDAY
	1	**2**	**3**
7	**8**	**9**	**10**
14	**15**	**16**	**17**
21	**22**	**23**	**24**
28	**29**	**30**	

JULY 2022

SUN	MON	TUE	WED	THU	FRI	SAT
					1	2
3	4	5	6	7	8	9
10	11	12	13	14	15	16
17	18	19	20	21	22	23
24	25	26	27	28	29	30
31						

AUGUST 2022

SUN	MON	TUE	WED	THU	FRI	SAT
	1	2	3	4	5	6
7	8	9	10	11	12	13
14	15	16	17	18	19	20
21	22	23	24	25	26	27
28	29	30	31			

SEPTEMBER 2022

SUN	MON	TUE	WED	THU	FRI	SAT
				1	2	3
4	5	6	7	8	9	10
11	12	13	14	15	16	17
18	19	20	21	22	23	24
25	26	27	28	29	30	

OCTOBER 2022

SUN	MON	TUE	WED	THU	FRI	SAT
						1
2	3	4	5	6	7	8
9	10	11	12	13	14	15
16	17	18	19	20	21	22
23	24	25	26	27	28	29
30						

NOVEMBER 2022

SUN	MON	TUE	WED	THU	FRI	SAT
		1	2	3	4	5
6	7	8	9	10	11	12
13	14	15	16	17	18	19
20	21	22	23	24	25	26
27	28	29	30			

DECEMBER 2022

SUN	MON	TUE	WED	THU	FRI	SAT
				1	2	3
4	5	6	7	8	9	10
11	12	13	14	15	16	17
18	19	20	21	22	23	24
25	26	27	28	29	30	

*OCT 2022

NOTE

SUNDAY	MONDAY	TUESDAY
2	3	4
9	10	11
16	17	18
23	24	25
30	31	

- ○
- ○
- ○
- ○
- ○
- ○
- ○
- ○
- ○
- ○

JANUARY 2021
SUN	MON	TUE	WED	THU	FRI	SAT
						1
2	3	4	5	6	7	8
9	10	11	12	13	14	15
16	17	18	19	20	21	22
23	24	25	26	27	28	29
30	31					

FEBRUARY 2022
SUN	MON	TUE	WED	THU	FRI	SAT
		1	2	3	4	5
6	7	8	9	10	11	12
13	14	15	16	17	18	19
20	21	22	23	24	25	26
27	28					

MARCH 2022
SUN	MON	TUE	WED	THU	FRI	SAT
		1	2	3	4	5
6	7	8	9	10	11	12
13	14	15	16	17	18	19
20	21	22	23	24	25	26
27	28	29	30	31		

APRIL 2022
SUN	MON	TUE	WED	THU	FRI	SAT
					1	2
3	4	5	6	7	8	9
10	11	12	13	14	15	16
17	18	19	20	21	22	23
24	25	26	27	28	29	30

MAY 2022
SUN	MON	TUE	WED	THU	FRI	SAT
1	2	3	4	5	6	7
8	9	10	11	12	13	14
15	16	17	18	19	20	21
22	23	24	25	26	27	28
29	30	31				

JUNE 2022
SUN	MON	TUE	WED	THU	FRI	SAT
			1	2	3	4
5	6	7	8	9	10	11
12	13	14	15	16	17	18
19	20	21	22	23	24	25
26	27	28	29	30		

WEDNESDAY	THURSDAY	FRIDAY	SATURDAY
			1
5	6	7	8
12	13	14	15
19	20	21	22
26	27	28	29

JULY 2022
SUN	MON	TUE	WED	THU	FRI	SAT
					1	2
3	4	5	6	7	8	9
10	11	12	13	14	15	16
17	18	19	20	21	22	23
24	25	26	27	28	29	30
31						

AUGUST 2022
SUN	MON	TUE	WED	THU	FRI	SAT
	1	2	3	4	5	6
7	8	9	10	11	12	13
14	15	16	17	18	19	20
21	22	23	24	25	26	27
28	29	30	31			

SEPTEMBER 2022
SUN	MON	TUE	WED	THU	FRI	SAT
				1	2	3
4	5	6	7	8	9	10
11	12	13	14	15	16	17
18	19	20	21	22	23	24
25	26	27	28	29	30	

OCTOBER 2022
SUN	MON	TUE	WED	THU	FRI	SAT
						1
2	3	4	5	6	7	8
9	10	11	12	13	14	15
16	17	18	19	20	21	22
23	24	25	26	27	28	29
30	31					

NOVEMBER 2022
SUN	MON	TUE	WED	THU	FRI	SAT
		1	2	3	4	5
6	7	8	9	10	11	12
13	14	15	16	17	18	19
20	21	22	23	24	25	26
27	28	29	30			

DECEMBER 2022
SUN	MON	TUE	WED	THU	FRI	SAT
				1	2	3
4	5	6	7	8	9	10
11	12	13	14	15	16	17
18	19	20	21	22	23	24
25	26	27	28	29	30	31

*Nov 2022

SUNDAY	MONDAY	TUESDAY
		1
6	**7**	**8**
13	**14**	**15**
20	**21**	**22**
27	**28**	**29**

NOTE

- ○
- ○
- ○
- ○
- ○
- ○
- ○
- ○
- ○
- ○

JANUARY 2021						
SUN	MON	TUE	WED	THU	FRI	SAT
						1
2	3	4	5	6	7	8
9	10	11	12	13	14	15
16	17	18	19	20	21	22
23	24	25	26	27	28	29
30	31					

FEBRUARY 2022						
SUN	MON	TUE	WED	THU	FRI	SAT
		1	2	3	4	5
6	7	8	9	10	11	12
13	14	15	16	17	18	19
20	21	22	23	24	25	26
27	28					

MARCH 2022						
SUN	MON	TUE	WED	THU	FRI	SAT
		1	2	3	4	5
6	7	8	9	10	11	12
13	14	15	16	17	18	19
20	21	22	23	24	25	26
27	28	29	30	31		

APRIL 2022						
SUN	MON	TUE	WED	THU	FRI	SAT
					1	2
3	4	5	6	7	8	9
10	11	12	13	14	15	16
17	18	19	20	21	22	23
24	25	26	27	28	29	30

MAY 2022						
SUN	MON	TUE	WED	THU	FRI	SAT
1	2	3	4	5	6	7
8	9	10	11	12	13	14
15	16	17	18	19	20	21
22	23	24	25	26	27	28
29	30	31				

JUNE 2022						
SUN	MON	TUE	WED	THU	FRI	SAT
			1	2	3	4
5	6	7	8	9	10	11
12	13	14	15	16	17	18
19	20	21	22	23	24	25
26	27	28	29	30		

WEDNESDAY	THURSDAY	FRIDAY	SATURDAY
2	3	4	5
9	10	11	12
16	17	18	19
23	24	25	26
30			

JULY 2022
SUN	MON	TUE	WED	THU	FRI	SAT
					1	2
3	4	5	6	7	8	9
10	11	12	13	14	15	16
17	18	19	20	21	22	23
24	25	26	27	28	29	30
31						

AUGUST 2022
SUN	MON	TUE	WED	THU	FRI	SAT
	1	2	3	4	5	6
7	8	9	10	11	12	13
14	15	16	17	18	19	20
21	22	23	24	25	26	27
28	29	30	31			

SEPTEMBER 2022
SUN	MON	TUE	WED	THU	FRI	SAT
				1	2	3
4	5	6	7	8	9	10
11	12	13	14	15	16	17
18	19	20	21	22	23	24
25	26	27	28	29	30	

OCTOBER 2022
SUN	MON	TUE	WED	THU	FRI	SAT
						1
2	3	4	5	6	7	8
9	10	11	12	13	14	15
16	17	18	19	20	21	22
23	24	25	26	27	28	29
30						

NOVEMBER 2022
SUN	MON	TUE	WED	THU	FRI	SAT
		1	2	3	4	5
6	7	8	9	10	11	12
13	14	15	16	17	18	19
20	21	22	23	24	25	26
27	28	29	30			

DECEMBER 2022
SUN	MON	TUE	WED	THU	FRI	SAT
				1	2	3
4	5	6	7	8	9	10
11	12	13	14	15	16	17
18	19	20	21	22	23	24
25	26	27	28	29	30	31

*DEC 2022

NOTE

SUNDAY	MONDAY	TUESDAY
4	5	6
11	12	13
18	19	20
25	26	27

JANUARY 2021						
SUN	MON	TUE	WED	THU	FRI	SAT
						1
2	3	4	5	6	7	8
9	10	11	12	13	14	15
16	17	18	19	20	21	22
23	24	25	26	27	28	29
30	31					

FEBRUARY 2022						
SUN	MON	TUE	WED	THU	FRI	SAT
		1	2	3	4	5
6	7	8	9	10	11	12
13	14	15	16	17	18	19
20	21	22	23	24	25	26
27	28					

MARCH 2022						
SUN	MON	TUE	WED	THU	FRI	SAT
		1	2	3	4	5
6	7	8	9	10	11	12
13	14	15	16	17	18	19
20	21	22	23	24	25	26
27	28	29	30	31		

APRIL 2022						
SUN	MON	TUE	WED	THU	FRI	SAT
					1	2
3	4	5	6	7	8	9
10	11	12	13	14	15	16
17	18	19	20	21	22	23
24	25	26	27	28	29	30

MAY 2022						
SUN	MON	TUE	WED	THU	FRI	SAT
1	2	3	4	5	6	7
8	9	10	11	12	13	14
15	16	17	18	19	20	21
22	23	24	25	26	27	28
29	30	31				

JUNE 2022						
SUN	MON	TUE	WED	THU	FRI	SAT
			1	2	3	4
5	6	7	8	9	10	11
12	13	14	15	16	17	18
19	20	21	22	23	24	25
26	27	28	29	30		

WEDNESDAY	THURSDAY	FRIDAY	SATURDAY
	1	2	3
7	8	9	10
14	15	16	17
21	22	23	24
28	29	30	31

JULY 2022

SUN	MON	TUE	WED	THU	FRI	SAT
					1	2
3	4	5	6	7	8	9
10	11	12	13	14	15	16
17	18	19	20	21	22	23
24	25	26	27	28	29	30
31						

AUGUST 2022

SUN	MON	TUE	WED	THU	FRI	SAT
	1	2	3	4	5	6
7	8	9	10	11	12	13
14	15	16	17	18	19	20
21	22	23	24	25	26	27
28	29	30	31			

SEPTEMBER 2022

SUN	MON	TUE	WED	THU	FRI	SAT
				1	2	3
4	5	6	7	8	9	10
11	12	13	14	15	16	17
18	19	20	21	22	23	24
25	26	27	28	29	30	

OCTOBER 2022

SUN	MON	TUE	WED	THU	FRI	SAT
						1
2	3	4	5	6	7	8
9	10	11	12	13	14	15
16	17	18	19	20	21	22
23	24	25	26	27	28	29
30	31					

NOVEMBER 2022

SUN	MON	TUE	WED	THU	FRI	SAT
		1	2	3	4	5
6	7	8	9	10	11	12
13	14	15	16	17	18	19
20	21	22	23	24	25	26
27	28	29	30			

DECEMBER 2022

SUN	MON	TUE	WED	THU	FRI	SAT
				1	2	3
4	5	6	7	8	9	10
11	12	13	14	15	16	17
18	19	20	21	22	23	24
25	26	27	28	29	30	31

Hi,
We created this book to help you with BEEKEEPING!
We hope you love it! If you do, would you consider posting an online review on AMAZON!
This helps us to continue providing great products and helps potential buyers to make confident decisions,
Thank you in advance for your review and for being a preferred customer.

Good luck :)

Printed in Poland
by Amazon Fulfillment
Poland Sp. z o.o., Wrocław
18 November 2021

83abc1d7-e70d-4fe5-b441-47fe267d1f32R01